Parasocial Romantic
Relationships

Parasocial Romantic Relationships

Falling in Love with Media Figures

Riva Tukachinsky Forster

LEXINGTON BOOKS

Lanham • Boulder • New York • London

Published by Lexington Books
An imprint of The Rowman & Littlefield Publishing Group, Inc.
4501 Forbes Boulevard, Suite 200, Lanham, Maryland 20706
www.rowman.com

6 Tinworth Street, London SE11 5AL, United Kingdom

British Library Cataloguing in Publication Information Available

Library of Congress Control Number: 2021934267

ISBN 978-1-7936-0958-8 (cloth)
ISBN 978-1-7936-0960-1 (pbk)
ISBN 978-1-7936-0959-5 (electronic)

Contents

Preface

A PERSONAL INTRODUCTION—FROM
MY FIRST LOVE TO THIS BOOK

Like much (of good) research, the endeavor behind this project is, in essence, a *ME*search. It is a quest for self-understanding. The scientist explores socially significant questions using rigorous scientific methods, thereby expanding the body of knowledge in the discipline and advancing understanding of some aspect of human behavior. However, this research also illuminates a hidden corner of the researcher's own psyche.

So let me share a secret with you. My first true love was MacGyver. Not the arrogant high-tech youngster from the 2016 reboot of the show, but the real MacGyver, portrayed by Richard Dean Anderson in the late 1980s and early 1990s. MacGyver was the most handsome man in the world, singularly sensitive, ingenious, incredibly creative, and a pacifist (except in the pilot episode, he would never fire a gun). It therefore stands to reason that I—then an elementary school girl—was enchanted by him. I fantasized about MacGyver coming to rescue me and taking me with him someplace where we would live until I grew up and could marry him. Some two decades later, when I found myself spending sleepless nights nursing a colicky baby, a DVD rental service rekindled my erstwhile relationship with MacGyver (i.e., after I got past the flat acting, the laughable dialogue, and the horrid fashion). I jokingly justified my renewed obsession with scientific evidence (e.g., Schneiderman et al. 2012, 1281) suggesting that being in love and interacting with one's romantic partner stimulates the release of oxytocin—a hormone that is also known to facilitate lactation.

As a media psychology scholar, I am fascinated with the human ability to be so profoundly moved by what we know to be unreal. Over the years, researching people's emotional responses to media has become my career. In my research, I have used theories of communication and social and cognitive psychology to understand how and why people are attracted to media content, relate to media characters, and become engrossed in narratives. I have looked at the impact that these cognitive and emotional experiences may have on media users' psychological well-being, attitudes, and behaviors in a variety of domains, from social stereotyping to engaging in precautionary health actions. Audiences' romantic feelings toward media personalities continue to be one of the questions about which I am most curious about.

At the time I started exploring romantic attachment to media figures, there was a paucity of research and theorization about this phenomenon. In the second decade of the new millennium, things began to shift, and I watched how this topic started enjoying an upsurge in research interest. Yet, many questions remained unanswered. This book is an effort to take another step toward filling this void by summarizing what is already known, providing some (even tentative) answers to questions that have been understudied thus far, and outlining a blueprint for possible directions for future investigation.

THIS BOOK

This book is a culmination of several research projects. First, it traces histori-cal examples of media users' experiences with media figures and documents the sociocultural context in which they appeared. Second, I report results from previously published work and reanalyze data that I have collected together with my colleague, Dr. Sam Dorros (Tukachinsky and Dorros 2018). Our stud-ies include a survey of college students and a survey of adolescents ages 13–17 across the United States. Third, specifically for the purpose of this book, I have conducted a national survey of Americans matched to the general population on key demographic characteristics. Fourth, I have interviewed individuals who have had a romantic experience with media figures. The aim of these in-depth interviews was to pry deeper into the lived experiences of romantic engagement with media. The methodological appendix provides a description of the survey and in-depth interviews conducted for the purpose of this book and the ques-tions used to assess these media-based fanciful romantic relationships. The data collected using these diverse methodological approaches are woven together to shed light on the phenomenon of romantic engagement with media figures.

The Book's Structure

The first chapter defines romantic experience with media figures and situates this phenomenon within a broader context of audiences' engagement with people in the media and in the nonmediated social realms. The scope of the book encompasses experiences such as crushes, romantic feelings, infatuation, and romantic attachment. The target of these feelings can be anyone in the media—from social media influencers to music artists, Hollywood actors, and entirely fictional characters appearing in novels and starring in television series. While being a devoted fan of a music artist and being in love with a cartoon character may sound like categorically different types of experiences, the first chapter suggests that they are actually not that distinct, and in fact, both closely resemble nonmediated relationships.

As demonstrated through multiple historical examples in the second chapter of the book, romantic interest in media figures is not a new or rare occurrence. Documentation of these experiences dates back to antiquity and constitutes an integral part of today's culture, propagated through strategic media industry practices. In the third chapter, historical and contemporary data from various sources are used to ascertain the prevalence of this phenomenon and paint a portrait of individuals who are most likely to develop romantic relationships with media figures and the attributes of these media targets.

Once a relationship between an audience member and a media figure is established, it is sustained through various practices. However, naturally, much of the regular repertoire of relational maintenance behaviors that people employ in their social relationships does not apply to relationships that are one-sided. Building on research on relationships during lack of co-presence (e.g., long-distance relationships), the fourth chapter offers a new understanding of how relationships with media figures are maintained. Although imagination lies at the core of romantic media experiences with media figures, to date, little has been uncovered about the actual content of these fantasies. To address this question, the fourth chapter reports results from in-depth interviews to provide a first look into the ways fanciful romantic experiences are carried out.

The following two chapters discuss possible theoretical explanations as to why people romantically engage with media figures (chapter 5) and provide evidence of the effects that they may have on media users' beliefs and subsequent romantic experiences (chapter 6). The book makes a particular effort to shed light on some questions that have been largely overlooked in the existing published body of scholarship. First, past research has not addressed the singular role of these experiences for LGBT individuals. Thus, special consideration is given to same-sex romantic experiences in chapter 7. Second, while most of the studies in this field focus on adolescents' engagement with media celebrities, the research presented in this book demonstrates that romantic attachment to media figures occurs across the life span. Uniquely, chapter 8 fleshes out the varying roles that they play in different life stages and at various transitional points in life.

Given the historical context in which fandom and romantic feelings toward media figures have often been stigmatized and have become culturally associated with mental health deficits, the book also discusses the line between normalcy and pathology (chapter 9). The book concludes with a discussion of the dissolution of fanciful romantic relationships with media figures. Chapter 10 considers the many ways in which a breakup between an audience member and a media figure can take place, from the sudden death of the media figure, to a gradual outgrowing of the relationship, to a media-user-initiated breakup in response to the media figure's reprehensible behavior.

While the book does not provide a complete and definitive answer to the questions it raises, it does take an important step toward understanding some understudied aspects of romantic engagement with media personalities. The concluding chapter offers a research agenda, outlining areas that need to be addressed by future research. In so doing, the book offers insights related to broader questions concerning the psychology of media effects, audience engagement with media, social daydreaming, and adolescents' sexual development. Going beyond the purely scholarly and academic context, I also hope that this project provides readers with greater self-understanding, especially for those who, like me, have experienced PSRRs firsthand.

Acknowledgments

I want to express my gratitude to the many individuals without whom it would have been impossible for me to complete this book. I am fortunate to be a faculty member at Chapman University, an institution that values and facilitates research and student–faculty collaboration. I am grateful for the School of Communication for providing me with the institutional support that enabled me to complete this book. I want to thank the Chapman University students who worked with me over the past years, assisting with coding data for the quantitative content analysis, recruiting study participants, and transcribing interviews. I also want to thank my colleagues, friends, and students who read and commented on early drafts of this book. I especially want to acknowledge my friend and colleague Dr. Sam Dorros, who has collaborated with me on an earlier research project on the same topic that is cited in this book. Special thanks go to Nina Conrad for the copyediting work. Finally, I am most grateful to the supportive and encouraging team at Lexington Books, particularly my editor Jessica Tepper and the anonymous reviewer who offered exceptionally thoughtful feedback that made the book much stronger, Baruch HaShem.

Chapter 1

Imaginary Love Is Real

"How could he do this to me?" cried Eliz. "I cannot believe he married her!"

I searched for words to comfort my best friend but could not find any. How could I tell Eliz that he had not done it to *her*? Eliz was a seventh-grade student and they had never met in person. In fact, he did not even know about her existence. Obviously, Michael Jackson's marriage to Lisa Presley did not make my friend's odds of marrying him any lower than they were to begin with. Yet none of these arguments would have been helpful at that moment, so I bit my tongue and offered Eliz the tissue box again as she sobbed, "He cannot truly love her. They will break up, I know!"

Eliz's relationship with Michael Jackson existed entirely in her imagination. In fact, the Michael Jackson she was in love with was not the actual person he was but a fictional persona she constructed in her mind based on his media image. Nonetheless, clearly, Eliz's feelings for Michael Jackson were real, deep, and meaningful, and so were her pain and jealousy. In essence, her romantic relationship *was*, in fact, real. It was just *parasocial*.

DEFINING PARASOCIAL ROMANTIC RELATIONSHIPS

Parasocial means quasi-social. Parasocial relationships (PSRs) do not occur in the social world but in one's imagination, yet they resemble nonmediated social relationships in their psychological makeup. It is nearly impossible to talk about "social relationships" overall because they encompass a wide range of qualitatively very different experiences—your mother, your best friend, a coworker, a boss, a romantic partner, the mail courier who has delivered post to your address every day for the past 5 years—they all represent social relationships, but each possesses unique characteristics. Similarly, it has been pointed out that PSRs can be classified into various types of fanciful bonds. Some people relate to media personalities as if they were parent figures or mentors (Stever 2009), and other PSRs resemble a friendship or romance (Tukachinsky 2011).

The focus of this book is on parasocial romantic relationships (PSRRs), which range from celebrity crushes to falling in love with fictional characters in a novel. Paralleling the definition of nonmediated romantic love (Feeney, Noller, and Roberts 2000, 187–8; Hendrick and Hendrick 2000, 204, 209–10), PSRRs are a form of passionate love that comprises two major facets: (1) a physical dimension, including attraction, lust, and sexuality, and (2) an emotional dimension that entails seeking intimacy, seeing the media figure as one's soulmate, a desire to be in unity with him or her, and deeply empathizing with the media figure (Tukachinsky 2011).

Like every PSR, PSRRs have affective, cognitive, and behavioral manifestations (Tukachinsky and Stever 2019, 299). First, on the affective level, media users can experience strong feelings toward the celebrity or the character, such as attraction, lust, and longing. Second, the cognitive aspect of the PSRR involves fantasizing about the media figure. For example, the media user may daydream about spending time together with the media personality, generating imaginary scenarios about their relationship. Finally, behavioral manifestation of PSRRs involve consuming media content featuring the target of the PSRR, trying to contact the media figure (e.g., by attending fan meet-and-greet events and fan conferences), collecting memorabilia, and searching for information about the object of the parasocial love.

WHAT PARASOCIAL ROMANTIC
RELATIONSHIPS ARE NOT

It is easy to confuse PSRRs with other forms of involvement with media figures. Thus, it may be helpful to draw the boundaries between PSRRs and other related concepts. First, both PSRs and PSRRs can have a very broad range of targets, including both real and imaginary media personality. Conversely, the focus of theories of celebrity admiration is on situations in which the target of the romantic ideation is a real personality such as a music artist. As such, these theories are less suitable to studying imaginary romantic relationships with fictional beings. Although (as will be discussed in chapter 3) the line between characters and the actors that play them may become somewhat blurry, at least some of the time, audience members do maintain a clear distinction between the two and can have a PSRR with the fictional character, not the actor. Moreover, at times, the fictional character may have no real-life referent altogether, such as in the case of literary or cartoon (e.g., anime) characters. While lying outside the scope of celebrity research, the bond with such fictional being would fall within the realm of PSRRs.

On a conceptual level, phenomena such as fandom, celebrity admiration, celebrity worshiping, and idealization are theorized to be a subset, or a sub-type, of PSRs (Giles 2010, 447). PSRs can involve many other qualitatively and quantitatively different ways of relating to media personalities, including friendship and parental attachment (e.g., Stever 2009). Moreover, PSRs may not rise to the level of fandom and do not necessarily involve idealization and worshiping (Tukachinsky and Stever 2019, 300, 305-307). Considering more specifically the distinction between PSRRs and fandom, it is true that sexual attraction can be a catalyst of fandom. For example, Stever (1991, 863) found that sexual appeal explained over 60% of the variance in fans' dedication to Michael Jackson. However, although fandom can, it does not necessarily involve romantic undertones or sexual infatuation.

When I have interviewed individuals about their PSRRs, many used the word "obsessed" to describe their relationship with the media figure with whom they had an imaginary relationship. When I asked them how this "obsession" was different from "just regular fandom" or "being a fan," the informants sometimes struggled to articulate the distinction even though it was obvious to them. Surely, there was an element of sexual attraction, but the difference had something to do with the specific hues of the emotions they harbored toward the media figure. Two words emerged as they attempted to describe the specific nature of these emotions, "fondness" and "attachment," which clearly reflected the emotional facet of parasocial romance. Breanna (interview #7) elaborated on this sense of intimacy:

> He was like a safe space, like a comfort person, like the one person that I was very dependent on to make myself feel better and it was just like a connection that you have with no one else.

Similarly, after Damian (interview #17) expressed his sexual attraction to a media figure, he stressed that what sets this experience aside from mere attraction is that it also involves a "fuzzy feeling inside and it's something [. . .] like I have a connection or relation to. [T]his feels deeper, this feels like somebody I've connected with already." Moreover, unique to PSRRs, my interviewees stated that one way or another, they wished they could be the media figure's romantic partner or become a couple with the media figure's clone. These feelings of "fondness," "obsession," "attachment," and "con-nection," coupled with sexual attraction, map onto the emotional and physi-cal dimensions of PSRRs. Although such psychological reactions to media figures can occur as part of fandom more broadly, they are not the focus of fandom and celebrity research, but they constitute the centerpiece of PSRRs.

Hence, traditional fan theories and research do not specifically examine fans' romantic attachment to media figures (e.g., Booth 2018).

BETWEEN REAL AND UNREAL

How can people develop such strong feelings toward people they do not actually know, probably have never met, and are unlikely to meet in the future? In the case of PSRRs with fictional characters, the object of one's romantic love does not even exist at all, leaving no hope for a real-life encounter. Yet, in full awareness of the fact that the character is the fruit of a scriptwriter's or novelist's imagination, otherwise smart and rational individuals develop deep, meaningful feelings toward these media figures. How come? How is it even possible for people to carry out entire relationships in their imagination without any reciprocation from the object of their love? The answers to these questions lie in the fuzzy distinction between real and unreal and the perhaps surprising ways in which the human brain processes the two.

The Unreal Is Real

Sure, people can tell the difference between a real thing and its representation in the media. Even children as young as 4 to 5 years old start recognizing the difference between real and media-reality (e.g., Mares and Sivakumar 2014). But on some level, we actually do not make this distinction. In evolutionary terms, symbolic communication, such as movies and even novels, has not existed long enough for the human brain to develop unique brain structures responsible for processing media-based characters and objects (Jacobs and Willems 2018, 148). Rather, the same brain processes involved in decoding information from one's actual environment are also used to process whatever happens in the media environment (Reeves and Nass 1996, 12; Stever 2017, 96). These primal processes that do not differentiate between real and unreal trigger immediate emotional reactions. Only milliseconds later do higher level, more advanced cortical processes call off the alarm, declaring the object "unreal." This is an adaptive response, as it is usually better to err on the side of overreacting to a false threat than ignoring a real one. When encountering a potential danger, starting to analyze, theorize, and ponder upon it before reacting would be maladaptive. By the time one decides on the best-fitting course of action, it may be too late. Those who have survived to pass on their genes are those who reacted first and thought second. It is better to discover later that a snake was just a picture than to not respond in time to a real snake.

And so, when people see a picture of a snakelike object, even if very briefly, the brain immediately mobilizes the body to fight or flee the danger (Öhman and Soares 1993). Meanwhile, the information continues to be processed and the alarm is shut down. This is why spectators do not jump onto the stage to prevent Hamlet from committing a murder and do not shatter their TV screen in attempts to kill a snake in a National Geographic documentary or an *Indiana Jones* film. However, even though the real–unreal distinction happens quickly, in a matter of milliseconds, by the time the determination has been made, the emotional and physiological cascade has already been triggered. Hormones have been released into the bloodstream and now circulate in the body, speeding up the heartbeat, making the palms sweat, and giving a feeling of butterflies in the stomach. These emotions are, therefore, as real as emotions elicited by the real object rather than its media representation. This is, for example, why scary media content, even when people are well aware of its fictional status, can leave lingering traumatic effects similar to what witnessing the depicted event in a nonmediated world would have produced (Cantor 2006, 321–322).

Once the distinction between real and unreal has been made, the media consumers may opt to suspend their disbelief. This is to say, they can ignore, at least to an extent, the call to shut off the alarm in order to continue enjoying the media world as if it were real. In an unwritten contract between the audience and the creators of the media, readers and viewers are willing to accept the internal rules of fictional universes. Viewers accept the *Walking Dead* reality in which all humans carry a pathogen that predisposes them to turn into zombies, and they buy into the *Star Trek* reality in which one can be "beamed" (i.e., teletransported) but this capability is limited by thick layers of rocks, solar flares, and electromagnetic storms. These departures from real life (external realism) are not an obstacle to involvement. However, if the internal rules of the world are broken (e.g., with no logical explanation, a *Star Trek* character is beamed during an electromagnetic storm), media users find it hard to forgive and are forced to suspend their belief in the imaginary reality (Busselle and Bilandzic 2008). This explains why avid viewers of the *Game of Thrones* fantasy television series happily engage in heated debates over the best strategy for using dragons in combat, but they are enraged when a Starbucks paper coffee cup left on set is visible in a shot (Whitten 2019). Similarly, *Game of Thrones* viewers were outraged in the final season when characters acted in ways that defied everything they had stood for in previous seasons of the show (Blake 2019). Such violations of the internal rules of that fictional reality (which is assumed to have no Starbucks and in which viewers expect characters to act in certain ways) made viewers suspend their belief in that world. But until such violations occur, or until the media user makes a conscious decision to withdraw from the imaginary reality, the fantasy is experienced by the audience to be as authentic as the nonmediated reality is. Hence, even though typical audience members would not jump onto the stage, some 17% of television viewers report that they yell at characters onscreen ("Don't do that, Tony!" "Are you stupid?") and murmur comments such as "Aww, that was so sweet, Jesse" (Dibble and Rosaen 2011, 129).

The Real Is Unreal

The line between "real" and "unreal" becomes even more tantalizing when considering the fanciful aspects of relationships with individuals in our physical environment. Studies in different cultures consistently estimate that people spend between 30% and 60% of their waking time in daydreaming (for review, see Poerio and Smallwood 2016, 606). Social situations, particularly involving others whom the person knows in reality, make up as much as 70% to over 90% of these daydreams (Poerio et al. 2016, 6; Tuominen et al. 2019, 140). Chapter 4 discusses the crucial relational and psychological functions of the fanciful components of relationships, but for now, it is important merely to underscore how pervasive social daydreaming is. In fact, arguably, people spend more time interacting with others in their imagination than in actuality.

One core aspect of social daydreams involves generating and playing out imaginary scenarios of interactions with real-life friends, family members, and most commonly, romantic partners (Honeycutt 2014). These imaginary conversations can be retrospective, as in a reflection on past conversation, like replaying a mental record of the encounter, dwelling on how one could have handled the interaction differently. Other imaginary interactions are prospective, like a mental rehearsal of a script to be utilized in the future. For example, a person might imagine how he will kneel in a marriage proposal or, on the contrary, role-play a difficult breakup conversation in his head. In sum, imaginary interactions are pervasive and constitute an important building block of "real" relationships. Thus, the leap to having entirely one-sided, imaginary relationships with a media personality is not as much of a stretch as it may appear at first glance.

PARASOCIABILITY AS A CONTINUUM

Considering the differences between types of media figures with whom individuals form PSRs, Giles (2002) suggested that it is more useful to think of social/parasocial not as binary concept but as a continuum. On the one end of the continuum lie purely social, one-on-one relationships that are not mediated at all. As discussed earlier, even such close social relationships have a small fanciful component too. Some other social relationships have a larger parasocial component. Consider, for example, a junior in high school having a crush on the senior quarterback whom she has never spoken to but fantasizes about and watches from afar. From this perspective, a PSR with a professional athlete lies a little further on the parasocial continuum, and PSRs with fictional characters (followed by animated characters) rank as the most parasocial ones. Moreover, relationships may move along the continuum, potentially becoming more or less imaginary. For instance, when a media user meets a celebrity in person at a meet-and-greet event, or if the celebrity responds to the fan's comment on social media, a nonmediated relationship aspect to the relationship renders it less parasocial. If the two-sided interactions become more frequent, the relationship is no longer truly parasocial. Social media can facilitate such de-parasocialization. In a fairytale example that is planned to be adapted into a romantic comedy by Fox 2000, a college student used Twitter to ask out the professional tennis player Eugenie Bouchard. Bouchard agreed and followed through with her promise, transforming the PSR into a social one. Conversely, it took Danielle Caesar 5 years of social media following to get her celebrity crush—Disney actor Jake T. Austin—to start dating her. While those relationships did not last, it is not unprecedented for a celebrity to marry a fan. For example, at the age of 55, James Doohan, the actor best known for his role as Scotty in the television and film series *Star Trek*, married an 18-year-old fan. The marriage lasted until Doohan's death three decades later.

This book focuses on the various forms that PSRRs take, specifically with individuals that we meet through the media. However, it is not implausible that many of these notions could apply to other forms of romantic fantasies and "crushes" involving real-life targets, given that they too involve imaginary processes. PSRRs with media figures have a unique place not only psychologically but also within broader social and cultural contexts.

My childhood friend Eliz was just one 13-year-old girl who fantasized about getting cancer so that the Make-A-Wish Foundation would arrange for her to meet with Michael Jackson (and then he would fall in love with her, she would survive the cancer, and they would live happily ever after). However, her private romantic fantasy was fostered by large societal forces. These macro-level aspects of PSRRs are the focus of the following chapter. Then, the rest of the book turns back to explore the psychological properties of PSRRs: What makes some people more susceptible to PSRRs than others? Why do people seek out PSRRs? How do individuals handle them? What are the consequences of PSRRs? In what ways are they healthy (or not)?

Chapter 2

From Pinup Girls to Bieber Fever

In Western society, most people may think of romantic feelings and partner choice as fundamentally private affairs. However, love—how it is perceived and experienced—belongs to the collective arena as much as it is located in the personal sphere. Multiple cultural mechanisms embedded in economic interests and political systems work in orchestration to define, label, and attach value to emotions. They are then propagated through social norms, rituals, and symbolic artifacts that collectively construct and reproduce the romantic variant of love as the cultural default or ideal (Illouz 1997, 2–6).

Much the same way, PSRRs constitute a personal psychological experience, but they can also be considered a cultural practice situated within a broader social, economic, and even political context. To understand PSRRs as lying at the intersection of the intimate and the collective realms, it is vital to examine the role of social institutions that manufacture media personalities and then socialize the audiences into relating to media figures in a parasocial romantic way. To this end, this chapter explores the sociohistorical and economic mechanisms that gave rise to the emergence of PSRRs as a cultural phenomenon.

THE HISTORY AND SOCIOECONOMIC
CONTEXT OF PSRRS

How far back in human history do PSRRs go? Since PSSRs entail a connection between audiences and media figures, naturally, the intuitive answer is that PSRRs may originate with the conception of mass media in the broadest sense of the term. Perhaps one of the earliest mentions of PSRRs dates back to ancient Rome, occurring in the writings of the satirical poet Juvenal. In

Satire VI, Juvenal (2018) ridiculed women of his time for becoming infatuated with male celebrities. He concluded by warning his contemporaries that
they might be raising children fathered by their wives' idols (241):

Other women pay great prices for the favours of a comedian;
some will not allow Chrysogonus [a famous vocalist] to sing.
Hispulla has a fancy for tragedians;
but do you suppose that any one will be found to love
   Quintilian? [a famous rhetorician]
If you marry a wife, it will be that the lyrist Echion or Glaphyrus,
or the flute player Ambrosius, may become a father.
Then up with a long dais in the narrow street!
Adorn your doors and doorposts with wreaths of laurel, that your highborn son,
O Lentulus, may exhibit, in his tortoiseshell cradle,
 the lineaments of Euryalus or of a murmillo! [references to warriors and gladiators]

Unfortunately, only in the modern day do we have well-organized documentation of PSRR activities. Yet, the examination of the anecdotal accounts
of PSRRs across the entertainment industry at different points in history,
from Shakespearean theater to the age of MTV, reveals a similar pattern: discovering the economic potential behind PSRRs mobilizes the entertainment
industry to facilitate PSRRs.

One early example of the interplay between macro-level commercial and
industrial practices, PSRs, and PSRRs was observed by Oxford professor of
Shakespeare studies Emma Smith in her research on the sixteenth-century
theater industry in London. In her presentation (February 2019), Smith discussed how the rapidly evolving business practices of the theater were driven
at least in part by female fandom. Over the course of just three decades,
London went from having no purpose-built theaters in 1568 to as many as
seven of them in 1599. Unlike the sleazy, male-oriented outdoor theaters that
offered cheap entertainment, which women could not attend without being
suspected of easy virtue, indoor theaters offered a respectable, upper-class
entertainment experience. They may have even served as a leisure activity for
couples. Shortly, women came to occupy a major share of the total number
of theater patrons, and it is very likely that they had an impact on the shows
that were attended by couples. At the same time, actors become the chief
attraction that drew the audience, assuming the equivalent of today's celebrity status. Playwrights facilitated (or, perhaps exploited) this shift. In lieu of
allocating relatively equal parts to each member of the theatrical company,
playwrights started creating bigger, more dominant parts for actors who could
shine in roles that attract greater audiences. For instance, Richard Burbage,
the lead actor in Shakespeare's company, was famously appealing to women

spectators, to the point of being "chased" by women fans (Sae 2013, 67). Similarly, in the eighteenth century, English theater giants David Garrick and Sarah Siddons received fan letters, including ones professing love (Lilti 2017).

Lord Byron presents another vivid example of a literary celebrity target of PSRRs. The nineteenth-century poet is deemed one of the first clear examples of modern-day celebrities who received hundreds of fan letters, mostly from women who requested to remain anonymous. For example, one such letter was signed by a "Stranger" "whose heart you melt, and whose mind you vivify" (McDayter 2009, 135). These women professed their love to Byron and divulged romantic fantasies and ideations about him. Interestingly, some of them made it clear that they did not wish to consummate an actual relationship with him (in fact, a few turned down the opportunity to do so). Rather, they used him as a backdrop for daydreaming and imaginary romance—a "fulcrum for [the letter writer's'] imaginative life which she may project herself into endless scenarios that his imagined presence provides" (160). This was not the case for all women, of course. Some fans did seek Byron as a relational partner, and occasionally the PSRR even crossed the line into the social realm. Most notoriously, a fan mail exchange led Bryon to engage in an affair with Lady Caroline Lamb. However, when he decided to terminate the relationship she was unable to come to terms with the rejection and continued stalking him, making announced visits and even sending him pieces of her pubic hair (Tuite 2007). She then published the novel *Glenarvon*, which, behind the façade of fiction, recounted her relationship with Lord Byron. She went as far as to take a breakup letter that Byron had sent her and incorporate it in the novel as a letter written by the male character to the heroine (Tuite 2007, 73).

Byron's scandalous love life and the women's following were mobilized by his publishers to maximize revenue from his literary work. Byron and his agents carefully cultivated his sex appeal by circulating his portraits and inviting fans to engage with him. Consequently, as much as Byron was an influential poet, his legacy extends well beyond his art, marking the power of celebrity, female fandom, and mobilization of PSRRs for marketing and revenue.

The process of manufacturing a celebrity came to a pinnacle in twentieth-century cinema. Ironically, in the early days of the film industry, studios insisted on keeping actors anonymous. Presumably, this offered the studios greater control over the actors. Audiences, however, were infatuated with their favorite actors and overwhelmed studios with endless requests to reveal the actors' identities. In 1910, the Independent Moving Pictures Company gave in to the massive public pressure and released the name of one of its lead actresses, Florence Lawrence. By 1912, most studios had joined suit in making their actors' names public (Barbas 2001, 9–21). This led to the conception of the "Hollywood star system." Actors raised to star status went on tours and gave interviews, gossip magazines began to flourish, and fandom became the driving force of the motion picture economy. Movie marketing efforts shifted to center on the personas of the actors starring in the film, and entire departments were dedicated to constructing and maintaining actors' images (Gamson 2007, 5). As with theater, women patrons played a major role in the evolution of cinema. According to Barbas (2001, 60–63), women were more active, outspoken, and influential than male cinema fans, and by 1915 the movie industry became more woman-centered in its marketing strategies, specifically trying to appeal to and court female moviegoers. As part of this move, the novelist and screenwriter Elinor Glyn played a key role in cultivating the star status of her protégé, Rudolph Valentino. In so doing, she deliberately promoted an egalitarian sexual and romantic agenda, offering women a space for sexual and romantic fantasy (Horak 2010).

This is not a unique move. Arguably, the industry consistently employs various strategies to engage audiences and make content decisions that will please and compel the fan base. For instance, producers of media content may strategically hypersexualize characters (especially female characters) and include scenes portraying nudity or sexual activity as fodder for PSRR development. In anime and magna fandom, such practices have been dubbed "fan service" (Scott 2015, 179).

The industry also can manage media stars' romantic parasociability off-screen. For example, lavender marriage is a common practice wherein the media industry stages a heterosexual relationship or marriage to conceal a celebrity's lesbian/gay/bisexual status in fear that it would antagonize their fans. While some of these efforts stem from concerns of alienating conservative fans, lavender marriages also allow heterosexual fans to continue envisioning themselves as potentially viable mates with the celebrity. In a similar vein, the media industry may conceal a media figure's real-life romantic relationship, assuming that a single, romantically available media figure will promote greater PSRRs and better revenue. This, apparently, was the case for John Lennon, who married his college sweetheart, Cynthia, shortly before the Beatles raised to stardom. Brian Epstein, the Beatles' manager, strategized that the Lennons should hide their marriage from the public. Epstein reasoned that a lead singer who is not romantically available would compromise his efforts to grow the band's popularity (Puente 2015). More than half a century later, a friend of a Hollywood couple recounted a similar experience (personal communication, December 5, 2019). She told me that her childhood friend just started dating the actor when he landed his breakthrough role. The actor's manager dissuaded him from having his new girlfriend accompany him at a red-carpet event. The agent argued that introducing a girlfriend to audiences at this early stage of the actor's career would compromise his ability to generate traction from female fans who would be crucial for his future success. Maintaining the appearance of being single could increase his appeal and put him on a more successful career trajectory. Such calculated romantic parasociability was even used as a marketing technique in a tongue-in-cheek advertisement (figure 2.1).

Gender and PSRRs

The examples above repeatedly involve female fans engaging in PSRRs with male targets because these examples are best-documented. This image of women as overindulgent consumers is pervasive in popular culture and among early fandom researchers. In fact, this notion is rooted in the origins of the word "fan," which was derived from "fanaticism" in a religious context. Historically, women were long thought to be unable to tame their sexual drives and to have a greater (physiologically based) propensity for excessive devotion that enabled them to "indulge in [. . .] love-sick visions of heaven" (Leigh Hunt cited in McDayter 2009, p. 139). This susceptibility to fanaticism was then presumed to extend to secular contexts, such as the adoration of Richard Burbage and Lord Byron. In the twentieth century, while the movie industry encouraged women moviegoers, it also solidified the notion of fandom as a female behavior that is socially scrutinized. For example, the *New York Times* coverage of Rudolf Valentino's funeral singled out female fans stating that "some women were moved to tears" and "a woman and two girls were overcame" (Public Now Barred 1926, 5). The reporting elaborated on the three female fans who became particularly distraught (5). Similarly, although Shulman (1967, 21) reported that about 9,000 men and women passed Valentino's coffin, he chose to stress the isolated instances of women fainting (16) and female fans kissing Valentino through the coffin's glass lid (21). This reporting iconized female hysteria, showing that women, "like children [. . .] cannot resist the cinema's temptation. To the irrational and emotional females, it seemed, Valentino was as vivid and intimated as real life lover" (Barbas 2001, 170).

The common stereotype of PSRRs fits that notion of excessive devotion and overindulgence, particularly with younger female media users, rendering PSRRs an adolescent girl's behavior. However, it is important to remember that PSRRs do not spare men. For example, in the eighteenth and nineteenth centuries, women actors enjoyed their share of fan following too. The actresses' admirers were fueled not only by appreciation of the performers' art but also by sexual attraction (Nussbaum 2010, 57). Despite theaters' attempts to segregate audiences from actors and ban behind-the-scenes visitation (133), occasionally fandom relationships morphed from parasocial to

Figure 2.1 A 2016 Print Advertisement for a Norwegian Airline Makes a Tongue-in-cheek Reference to the Split between Hollywood Megastars Brad Pitt and Angelina Julie. Capitalizing on PSRRs with the Actor, the Airline Offered Discounted One-way Flights to the City Where the Newly Single Actor Resided. *Source:* Courtesy of TRY Advertising Oslo.

social, leading to affairs and occasionally even resulting in marriage (47). Whether PSRRs operate or function differently for men and women (as will be discussed more in chapter 3), several historical examples can speak to the cultural aspects of men's PSRRs, which involve many of the same social, economic, and even political forces.

The Lonesome Gal

Before there was *Sex and the City*, there was *The Lonesome Gal*—a radio show that started airing in 1947 and reached its peak in the early 1950s (Norris, n.d.). The program consisted of a one-person act in which an unnamed woman lamented about the loneliness of city life and found condolence in the imaginary company of her male listeners. Combining emotional intimacy with sexual innuendo, the actress directly addressed the listeners, delivering lines like, "You need someone to worry about you, who will look after your health, you need me, I share your hopes and your disappointments" (Horton and Wohl 1956, 224) and inviting the listener to lie by her side on the couch and let her stroke his hair.

The show became a national phenomenon. A local show in Dayton, Ohio, it was picked up and syndicated in over fifty stations across the United States (Norris, n.d.). Radio stations were showered with thousands of letters from men professing their love, expressing the belief that they and the Lonesome Gal were soulmates made for each other, and offering her their heart and hand (Horton and Wohl 1956, 224).

Notably, following the pattern described earlier with other media industries driven by female fandom, the producers maximized the traction of the show by carefully manipulating the media personality and building on her success. The show maintained strict confidentiality, never revealing the actress's identity and limiting her public appearances to just a single occasion, where she attended a public event wearing a mask. The show became a genre of its own, and new programs have been developed following the same format, arguably in order to maximize the profitable audience segment of single, upper-middle-class young men.

The story of the Lonesome Gal was recounted by Horton and Wohl (1956, 224) in their seminal paper that laid the foundation for PSR research. However, while this is perhaps the first example of male PSRRs documented in the PSR literature, other, well-studied social phenomena can also be interpreted as PSRRs. One example is the pinup cheesecake photography that evolved during World War II, just a few years before the Lonesome Gal captivated the romantic imagination of American men.

Cheesecake Girlfriends

Political figures were a source of inspiration and motivation for soldiers during the Civil War and World War I. But World War II was different. It was mobilized by "cheesecake photography"—racy pictures of young, typically scantily clad women in suggestive poses that were posted on the walls above soldiers' bunks and in their lockers. These images are not to be confused with pornography or erotic imagery per se. Unlike erotic and pornographic materials, cheesecake photography was deemed a desirable symbol of American womanhood. These women offered more than their looks. They provided inspiration and supported the troops' morale through fundraising activities, by entertaining soldiers at the frontlines, and by volunteering with soldiers' children.

From the soldiers' perspective, this was an opportunity to develop deeper imaginary intimacy with actresses whom they already knew from the big screen prior to the war. Some soldiers named aircraft and tanks after pinup girls such as Jane Russel, Rita Hayworth, and Ginny Simms. World War II also gave rise to *nose art*. Talented armature and professional artists who were drafted decorated the front sections of their aircraft with paintings of the likenesses of actresses to enhance aircrews' morale. These pinup girls afforded a fantasy escape from the traumatic realities of war and arguably served as a substitution for actual romantic relationships. They may even have offered consolation for lovelorn soldiers who were dumped by their girlfriends or wives. For example, the actress Janet Blair initiated a "love insurance policy," pledging to go on a date with a soldier who lost his girlfriend while fighting the war (Kiser 2013).

Importantly, although many of the pinup girl images are hypersexualized, they were not all about sex per se. For instance, Donna Reed supplied mostly farm-themed photos, such as pictures of herself modestly clad in shorts, milking cows. In so doing, she offered an idealized but not hypersexual image of womanhood that could be an object of a more romantic and less sexualized fantasy. This approach suited her well; in a poll conducted by the *Port Arthur News*, she was voted by soldiers as the "Girl we'd most like to come home to" (Kaiser 2013). Reed's estate included carefully kept dozens of letters she had received from the frontlines, decorated with romantically themed imagery (figure 2.2).

The pinup girl phenomenon during World War II has to be understood against the political background and within the economic context of the Hollywood industry. The pinup girl culture was a win-win for all parties involved: The government had to motivate the troops to take part in a war many did not care to understand. For actresses, the pinup phenomenon opened up new career paths. It provided breakthrough opportunities for aspiring actresses and facilitated the rise of established actresses from B-list to A-list status. Finally, thanks to the pinup culture's contribution to the war effort, Hollywood enjoyed laxer censorship. The moral code that Hollywood had to abide by prior to wartime was eased, and studios were free to cultivate a hypersexualized image for a noble cause in a feel-good way. The pinup

Figure 2.2 A Collection of Letters That Starstruck World War II Soldiers Mailed to the Actress Donna Reed. *Source:* Courtesy of *Librado Romero/The New York Times.*

girls' efforts were also strategically used to maximize publicity. For instance, the abovementioned Janet Blair's "love insurance policy" was mobilized to promote the actress's new movie *Two Yanks from Trinidad.*

Kiser (2013) argues that the media industry deliberately facilitated soldiers' illusion that their fantasy was reciprocated. The media did so by circulating rumors (mostly false) about pinup girls allegedly marrying servicemen. The rise of the pinup girl industry, then, was cultivated by joint commercial (movie industry) and political forces. These macro-level structures in turn generated individual-level fantasies and psychological experiences.

BRINGING IT ALL TOGETHER: INDUSTRY, SOCIETY, CULTURE

Considering the preceding examples, it is important to address the ways in which the celebrity industry and media in general work in tandem to enable, facilitate, and maintain PSRRs to promote economic (and possibly political) gains. Herman and Chomsky's (1988) propaganda model is an instrumental theoretical approach for understanding these processes. Although usually used to examine news, this framework is applicable to the media industry in a broader sense.

According to Herman and Chomsky, media content is distorted by several "filters," including the sources of media organizations' funding, the media's dependency on newsworthy sources, the media ownership structure, and spreading fear of political opponents.

The first filter is the media's sources of revenue. From this perspective, it is noteworthy that the media shift their marketing efforts from art (film, music, etc.) onto the artist's persona because this move is more profitable for the industry. As a rock music critic, Geoffrey Himes, quoted by Deena Weinstein (1999, 64) put it: "If record companies can get listeners to fall in love with the person rather than the song, there's a better chance fans will buy the next album—and concert ticket, T–shirt, video, book, and poster." The same logic equally applies to the theater, literature, and film industries. Capitalizing on the media personality increases the commercial value that can be extracted from the fans.

The second filter demonstrates how this interconnectedness is even more impactful due to the ownership of the media industry. Specifically, aggressive media consolidation trends over the past decades have fostered a growing interdependency between various media organizations. as the different media industries have become part of bigger conglomerates. Take for instance Walt Disney Inc.—one of the six major media giants that collectively produce over 80% of media content in the United States in the twenty-first century. In addition to movie production studios, Disney's assets include a major television network (ABC), cable channels (e.g., ESPN), streaming services (Hulu), several record labels, and print magazines for family and children. While for most media users these appear to be independent, unrelated media entities, they are in fact different arms of the same media conglomerate and thus share financial interests. It is, therefore, only to be expected that morning shows and network TV news will encourage their audience's devotion to an actor starring in a show on the conglomerate's streaming service or film produced in that media group's studio. The various forms of media work in orchestration to promote the star's brand, allowing the entire media industry to profit from a star-centered (rather than art-centered) marketing approach. Television talk show interviews and paparazzi photos in gossip magazines not only promote the movies that actors star in but also constitute a major stream of revenue for these television stations and magazines. This explains, for example, the remarkable cooperation between the different media industries, such as when magazines assisted in spreading (at times deliberately false) gossip vis-à-vis pinup girls' involvement in romantic relationships with military men.

This speaks to the third filter, sourcing. Various media outlets become increasingly reliant on each other for information. In the 1930s, Hollywood had already become one of the major sources of news (Gamson 2007, 6). This creates a symbiotic partnership between various media outlets that become increasingly dependent on each other.

Lastly, another filter of media content involves ideological opposition. According to Herman and Chomsky, there is an inherent connection between political structures and the media industry. At any point in time, they argue, the media are mobilized to spread fear against a common political rival. For instance, for the major part of the twentieth century, communism was a dreaded evil. At the turn of the century, Muslims became a new threat to the American social order. Media coverage of these issues has legitimized restrictions on personal freedoms (e.g., spying on citizens) and going to war against the Axis of Evil. Artists too play a role in this process, as seen in Ariana Grande's cancellation of her 2019 concert in Saudi Arabia to express her objection to the nation's abuses of human rights. The decision was widely publicized in the media, reinforcing a larger narrative critical of "Islamic extremists" in general and Saudi Arabia in particular. The cooperation between Hollywood and the US government that gave rise to the pinup girl culture in World War II falls neatly within this politically charged filter.

To conclude, this chapter provided a brief review of prominent instances of PSRRs from ancient times to this day and the roles that various social institutions play in facilitating these experiences. The following chapter offers a broader-strokes picture of how pervasive PSRRs are, looking at larger statistical trends beyond individual accounts of PSRRs.

Chapter 3

Who Falls in Love with Whom?

The previous chapter presented historical examples of audiences engaging in imaginary romantic relationships with media figures. It seems like PSRRs constitute an integral part of the culture. The first researchers to document PSRRs were Horton and Wohl (1956) in their seminal paper that coined the term "PSRs" and laid the foundation for this area of research. Although romantic PSRs were not the focus of their paper, to demonstrate the potential intensity of parasocial experiences, Horton and Wohl (315) reproduced a letter originally published in 1955 in Ann Landers's *Chicago Sun-Times* "Your Problems" advice column. In the letter, a 25-year-old female reader professed love of a local television star and sought counsel on how to manage her feelings, which were precluding her from dating men in her social circle. Today, one can find similar questions posted in online communities across the Internet.

"Is it weird to have crushes on book characters?" wondered a high school student after confessing developing feelings for Holden, the protagonist in *The Catcher in the Rye*, which she was assigned to read for class (Yahoo Answers n.d.). Other members of the online community responded to her post, reassuring her this is not uncommon and divulging their own romantic feelings toward various literary characters. PSRRs have become a staple of popular culture. Countless popular online memes make references to PSRRs. CeliaBowen's e-card reading "I don't care if he is a fictional character, I still want to marry him" (somecards.com n.d.) was even turned into a stylish T-shirt sold on Amazon. Print magazines and Internet websites publicize quizzes that supposedly test readers' romantic compatibility with various celebrities and fictional characters (e.g., "The Ultimate Celeb Boyfriend Quiz" in *Marie Claire*, 2015). In light-weight interviews, even celebrities in their own right are often asked about their current or early life celebrity crushes. In an interview on NBC Nightly News (2016 00:20), Simone Biles—a world-record-smashing Olympic gymnast—shared her infatuation with the actor Zac Efron. During the televised tour of her home, she showed off a life-size cutout of her celebrity crush. "Sometimes I used to kiss him on the cheek," Biles confessed.

Although there is no shortage of contemporary and historical examples of PSRRs, they amount to a collection of anecdotes. How prevalent are PSRRs on a societal level? How do we know that these stories are not cherry-picked, rare, and unrepresentative experiences? And what are the characteristics of these relationships? Who is most inclined to form PSRRs? With whom? And why? To shed light on these questions, this chapter reviews data derived from a number of sources, including fandom letters and surveys. Ideally, to accurately reflect the population, one needs data from a large, representative sample. Given that up until recently, research on PSRRs was very scant, to supplement past research findings I have conducted a survey of adult US Americans using a quota sample in which participants' key demographic characteristics are matched to those of the general population.

HOW COMMON ARE PSRRS?

One of the first archival research sources of information about PSRRs comes from research conducted by the UK sociologist Mayer in the 1940s. Mayer (1948) published an advertisement in the newspaper asking readers about their cinema-related habits, feelings, and experiences. The research corpus encompassed letters he received in response to this ad from 60 moviegoers. Obviously, this is a small and nonrepresentative sample, composed of 41 women and nineteen men. Their ages ranged from 15 to 47 (with a mean of 22.4 years). Most importantly, they were self-selected. Presumably, those who were eager to write the researcher and respond to questions about movies were more engaged and motivated than the average person on the street. Nonetheless, it is interesting to consider the prevalence of PSRRs in this sample. With the help of another coder, I have analyzed the 60 letters published in Mayer's book. Mayer's study was not about PSRRs, so the questions were not specific to this experience, but his prompts did offer an opportunity for readers to volunteer this information. Thus, whenever PSRRs were mentioned in the letter, we coded their characteristics. What we found was that the majority (41 of the letters; 68%) mentioned having a PSRR. Only twelve (20%) of the respondents explicitly stated they had not developed PSRRs, while the rest did not make any references to either having or not having PSRRs.

Different estimates can be drawn from research on fan mail. Leets, de Becker, and Giles (1995) surveyed college students about fandom letters they had written, then compared the results of the survey with an analysis of the fandom mail sent to a particular celebrity. The researchers found that only 3% of the fan letters made references to romantic and sexual themes (114). However, this could be an underestimate of the prevalence of PSRRs if those who experience it are not inclined to share their feelings in fan mail. Instead, it is possible that fans wish to share their advice, make requests, or express admiration overall rather than disclose their romantic feelings.

A different figure emerges from Dietz et al.'s (1991) analysis of fan mail. Their sample specifically included what they called "nut mail" (185), namely, fan mail that a security consultation firm had flagged as inappropriate (186). Over a quarter of those who wrote these letters cast themselves as a spouse/lover or a would-be spouse/lover of the celebrity (194, 200–1). Those who had attempted to approach the celebrity (e.g., invading the celebrity's property) were more likely to mention the desire to marry, have sex with, and bear children of the celebrity than those who did not make attempts to approach the celebrity (20% compared to just 6%). However, both groups often expressed sexual desire toward the celebrity (33% vs. 20%, respectively). While Dietz et al.'s estimates of the prevalence of PSRRs are markedly higher than those uncovered by Leets et al. (1995), obviously the discrepancy stems from the use of very different samples. While Leets looked at all fan mail, Dietz et al. specifically focused on "nut mail," which probably composes only a tiny fraction of fan mail overall.

More estimates of PSRRs' prevalence come from self-reported surveys. In a sample of 50 seventh- and ninth-grade girls in Israel, only one respondent did not have a media idol (Karniol 2001, 65). Similarly, Boon and Lomore (2001, 439) found in a survey of students from a large university in western Canada that 90% of the respondents had had an attachment (broadly defined) to a "celebrity idol" at some point in their lives, and roughly 75% of the respondents had had such an experience more than once. While these figures suggest that PSRRs are commonplace, it is important to note that they are limited to celebrities, leaving out PSRRs with other targets, such as fictional characters. At the same time, they do not always strictly define PSRRs and may, therefore, include other forms of engagement with media figures.

More accurate figures can be drawn from the data I collected with Dr. Sam Dorros (Tukachinsky and Dorros 2017, 2018). In that study, we specifically looked at PSRRs, asking whether the participants ever fell in love with, had a crush on, or had a romantic interest in a media figure. In a sample of 153 teenagers ages 13 to 17 from around the United States, the vast majority reported experiencing PSRRs: about half (49.7%) of the respondents said they had had such an experience once, and 22.9% had experienced multiple PSRRs. Clearly, PSRRs were not isolated cases but the norm.

Now that we have discussed the pervasiveness of PSRRs overall, we can turn to painting a portrait of the individuals who are most likely to develop PSRRs, the characteristics of the targets of their parasocial attraction, and their reasons for choosing these parasocial partners.

WHO DEVELOPS A PSRR?

A Teen Girl Thing?

As has been discussed in previous chapters, the prevailing stereotype casts PSRRs as a women's irrational, obsessive behavior typical of teenagers. Is it indeed strictly (or predominantly) an adolescent female phenomenon? Mayer's data from UK moviegoers in the 1940s show that both men and women experienced PSRRs. Overall, both of his samples were predominantly women (70% in his "sociology of film" survey and 68% in the "British cinemas" study). However, the share of women among those who reported a PSRR was similar to the share of respondents who did not have such a relationship. If anything, PSRRs were more prevalent in men (74% of male respondents) than women (65% of women respondents), although the differences were not statistically significant. However, in line with the stereotype, PSRRs do seem to be specific to adolescence in his sample (Mayer, 1948). Most respondents to Mayer's ad did not report the age when the PSRR occurred, but based on the description of those who did, the age of onset was as young as 8 and as old as 18 (with an average of 13.7).

More recently, Stever (2009, 14) examined the expression of different types of PSRs in interviews with fans, who were defined as such based on their engagement in one of the following activities: writing to celebrities, participating in fandom events attended by celebrities, being a member of a fan club, or having an extensive celebrity memorabilia collection. Her analysis of the fans' interviews suggests that the vast majority of both male (69%) and female (74%) fans experienced a romantic attachment to the celebrity; for example, referring to the celebrity's sex appeal or expressing a desire to marry the celebrity.

Similar conclusions emerge from my research that considers broader and more representative populations. In a survey of adolescents (Tukachinsky and Dorros 2018), although the share of participants who reported never having had a PSRR was slightly lower among girls than among boys (21.5% vs 32.4%, respectively) these differences were not statistically significant. Nor did boys and girls differ in the intensity or quality of their PSRRs. Teens, regardless of their gender, expressed very intense physical attraction to their PSRR targets (6.3 on a 7-point scale) and somewhat strong emotional connections (4.9 on a 7-point scale).

For this book, I have collected data from a national sample through an online survey provider (Qualtrics panels). In a sample of 566 individuals, 60.6% reported having had at least one PSRR. Intriguingly, the share of men who had had a PSRR (65.5%) was significantly higher than the percentage of women (56.6%) who had had a PSRR. Moreover, the intensity of the PSRR followed a similar pattern. Men experienced a stronger physical parasocial bond and marginally stronger emotional parasocial love. However, the level of communication and support was the same for men and women.

Other Media-User Characteristics

The national survey shows that PSRRs were common among all racial and ethnic groups. Interestingly, individuals who reported higher earnings were also more likely to have had a PSRR experience in the past. Respondents in the lowest income bracket were the least likely to have had a PSRR. For example, only 38.1% of individuals with an annual income of less than $10,000 had had a PSRR, and less than 60% of those earning between $10,000 and $50,000 reported having had a PSRR in the past. Similarly, although PSRRs were reported by individuals on all education levels, those who had had a PSRR tended to be slightly more educated. Importantly, however, even though the income and education groups differed significantly, overall, the percentage of individuals reporting a PSRR in their past was high across the board.

Finally, intriguingly, the respondent's current age was significantly related to the odds of having had a PSRR in the past. The average age of those who had ever had a PSRR was 44.84 years old, compared to 54.18 years for those who had never had a PSRR. In other words, younger people were more likely to have had a PSRR than older individuals. These effects (with the exception of education) remain significant when considered together in a logistic regression predicting the odds of having a PSRR. In other words, sex, income, and age were unique, significant predictors of having a PSRR.

Next, moving beyond PSRRs as a binary phenomenon, we can consider PSRRs' intensity. What characterizes people who form particularly strong parasocial romantic bonds? This time, of all the demographic characteristics, only sex and age were significant predictors of PSRR intensity. Specifically, males and younger respondents had stronger emotional PSRRs. Men also experienced stronger physical PSRRs (but there was no significant effect of age, and the effect of income was only marginal). I also asked respondents about factors related to their upbringing. The socioeconomic status of the family in which they grew up did not make a difference in the intensity of their subsequent PSRRs. However, the more important religion was in one's life growing up, the less intense was one's emotional (but not physical) PSRR.

Since these are cross-sectional data, it is important to interpret them with caution, without inferring causality. For example, these data alone do not indicate to what extent age differences in PSRR experiences are a function of a cohort effect, a developmental difference, or an artifact of self-reported data (chapter 8 explores these questions in more depth, considering PSRRs across the lifespan). Similarly, the intriguing relationship between PSRRs and the person's education and socioeconomic status needs further investigation. It is possible that the differences between PSRRs stem from other confounding factors, such as different social norms and leisure media use patterns. These limitations notwithstanding, the results of this survey, which was conducted on a relatively larger and more diverse sample than ones used in previous research, uniquely demonstrate the pervasiveness of PSRRs and indicate that they are certainly not limited to particular demographic niches. Moreover, the results of this survey resonate with the findings from earlier studies, dispelling the "crazed girl" fan stereotype.

Who Are the Targets of PSRRs?

Now, let's consider the characteristics of the media figures that serve as the objects of PSRRs. Who are these media figures, and what is it about them that attracts media users?

What Types of Media Figures?

In my studies, I have asked participants to indicate the type of media figure they engaged in a PSRR with (e.g., actor, music artist). If the media figure assumed more than one role, respondents were instructed to choose the role wherein they most related to the figure in. In a survey conducted for this book on a national sample of adults, half the participants were asked to recall their most meaningful PSRR while the other half reported about the most recent one. For both groups, the most common targets of PSRRs were actors (48.3% of the most recent PSRRs and 53% of the most meaningful PSRRs). There was a tremendous diversity of media figures named by the participants. Among the 343 responses, the most frequently mentioned media personalities included Tom Cruise and Farrah Fawcett (four mentions each) and Scarlett Johansson, Ryan Reynolds, and Johnny Depp (three mentions each). Actors were followed by music artists (18.4% of the most recent and 22.6% of the meaningful PSRRs). Here, the list of celebrities was more diverse, but Elvis

Presley was mentioned by four respondents. Few individuals (5–6%) had had a PSRR with a fictional character or athlete. The rest of the respondents listed "other" targets, mostly social media personalities such as YouTuber celebrities and Instagram influencers.

In the teenage sample (Tukachinsky and Dorros 2018), about half of the respondents listed music artists (54.5%; for example, Ariana Grande), who were followed in prevalence by actors (31.8%; for example, Emma Watson) and fictional character (10%; for example, Ross from *Friends*), and the rest listed athletes (3.6%; for example, John Cena). A somewhat different pattern was observed by Erickson and Dal Cin (2018, 123) in a sample of college women, 22% of whom reported fictional characters, such as Edward, the lead character from *Twilight* and Aragon from *Lord of the Rings*.

Notably, however, sometimes the lines between an actor and the fictional character they play are blurred. In a few instances, my survey respondents listed a fictional character (e.g., Chandler from *Friends*) but then in response to a multiple-choice item indicated a crush on the actor rather than the fictional character. The opposite happened too, with participants stating that they had a crush on a fictional character but then referring to the PSRR target by the actor's name (e.g., mentioning Jennifer Aniston in reference to Rachel, the fictional character she played on *Friends*).

The confusion between actors and characters is not unusual, as can be gleaned from similar anecdotal evidence that has been cited in past research. For example, fans playfully blended the actor's and the character's personas in their response to a kissing scene from the TV show *House M.D.* posted on YouTube. Some teenage girls posted comments sharing their romantic feelings toward Hugh Laurie—the actor playing Dr. House in that scene— but in the same breath referred to him in his fictional role. One of the fans exclaimed, "How can someone not love Hugh Laurie? He is sexy . . . and a doctor" (Tukachinsky 2010, 75). (figure 3.1).

Others have more directly acknowledged the twofold nature of their romantic attraction to the actor and the character. Reflecting on his PSRR with Luke Skywalker from *Star Wars*, *Washington Post* journalist and author Shane Harris spoke at length about Luke, then recognized, "I knew that he was a fictional character, and I also was drawn to the real person who played him in the movies: Mark Hamill" (Alter and Singleton 2016, 39). Demonstrating how the actor's and the character's persona blend, Harris recounted his feelings after the actor was involved in a serious car accident: "When I saw Luke in the *Empire Strikes Back* hooked up to tubes while a robot tended his wounds I imagined that's what Mark must have looked like in his real hospital room, damaged, vulnerable, fighting for life" (39–40).

Figure 3.1   UK Fans at a 2009 Twilight Saga Event, Blurring the Lines between the Actor's Persona and His Fictional Character of a Vampire. *Source:* Courtesy of WENN Rights Ltd.

The blending of the actor and the character seems to run even deeper. Sure, in our rational minds, starting around the age of 5 we become well aware of the difference between actors and the fictional roles they play as part of their jobs, and the ability to distinguish between reality and fiction reaches full fruition by the age of 11 (e.g., Mares and Sivakumar 2014). However, on more subconscious levels, this distinction becomes relatively blurry. For example, in an experiment, Tal Or and Papirman (2007) had high school students watch an episode from one of two fictional TV dramas featuring the same actor playing the leading role. One group of teenagers watched him play a negative character, whereas the other group watched a show in which he played a hero. When asked to reflect on the personality of the *actor*, study participants were inclined to rate the actor's traits as more aligned with the fictional character they observed him play. In other words, they projected the fictional character onto the actual persona of the actor. My own research yielded similar results (Tukachinsky 2020). I asked college students to watch one of two versions of an edited video featuring the same actress playing the role of either a positive or a negative character. Indeed, the way viewers perceived the *actress's* personality and their PSR with her were colored by whether they watched her play the villain or the protagonist. Moreover, when the students were later exposed to a public service announcement in which the same actress solicited donations to a research hospital, those who had watched the actress play the villain were more critical of the advertisement. For example, they claimed that the actress was duplicitous and disingenuous, and they were more cynical of her motives for participating in the ad. Conversely, those who watched the actress play a hero character stressed her good-heartedness and viewed her action as sincere. These studies suggest that media users do in fact conflate actors with characters and do not maintain a strict distinction between the two personas.

In the in-depth interviews that I conducted while working on this book, whenever a person described a PSRR with a fictional character or a movie star, I pressed to see how they experienced the actor–character duality. On some level, it appears, media users intuitively understand the actor–character fusion. For example, throughout one interview, Mika (interview #11) reflected on her crush on the lead character of the *Twilight* movies. When I asked her if it was the actor or the character that she was really attracted to, she described it as "kind of a mix" between the actor's media persona she constructs from information in interviews and the character she sees him portray in the move:

[I] would just kind of combine it together. [. . .] You can't tell the difference. [. . .] I'd say that the actor has to have to be portrayed in some way as to not ruin his character's good qualities. Like, if he's portrayed as violent [. . .], if I would read a newspaper article that says [. . .] "So-and-so is violent toward women" [. . .] it would destroy everything that I think about his character. I wouldn't be able to watch him being the romantic guy again, and [. . .] it would disgust me.

In reflecting on his media-based romantic experience as a teenager, Hunter (interview #15) similarly admitted to blending the fictional character Hermione Granger with Emma Watson, the actress who portrayed the character in the *Harry Potter* movie series:

I just think that [. . .] the idea that those were two separate things hadn't quite crystallized in my head yet. [. . .] I think I just took the best parts in my opinion, or like the things that I found the most desirable out of both, Hermione Granger and Emma Watson, and I just mashed them up into one dream girl. [. . .] I considered them one and the same, Hermione and Emma Watson. I was just, like, oh they're just the same thing.

WHAT ATTRACTS MEDIA USERS TO MEDIA FIGURES?

Consider the emblem of romantic love: Cupid armed with gold-pointed darts that induce an uncontrolled romantic desire in whoever they strike. This image embodies the notion of romantic love as unpredictable, illogical, capricious, and out of one's control. People just stumble into it—they *fall* in love.

As much as romantic love is culturally constructed as mysterious and unexplainable, for generations, social scientists have extensively examined romantic love. Psychologists and sociologists have searched for regularities, identified patterns, and made testable predictions trying to unearth the mechanisms of romantic love. What makes people fall in love with someone in particular and not with someone else? What attracts us to specific prospective partners and not to others? Trying to demystify the magic of initial romantic attraction, researchers have used various methods—from asking people to recall what they found attractive in their first encounter with their current romantic partner, to simulating an online dating experience and experimentally assessing the characteristics that increased the popularity of various prospective dates. Do the same principles of romantic attraction apply to PSRRs?

Among the characteristics uncovered in research on interpersonal romantic attraction, we can consider some environmental or incidental factors, such as proximity (which offers an opportunity for contact), similarity (actual or perceived) between oneself and one's partner, and physical attractiveness (e.g., Couch and Koeninger 2016). In particular, physical attractiveness has been found to be such a powerful predictor or romantic attraction that in statistical models predicting mate preferences, physical attraction overshadows any contribution of personality characteristics (Gerlach and Reinhard 2018, 2). However, it has been posited that evolutionary forces come into play, creating sex differences in the role of physique in mate selection (Couch and Koeninger 2016, 306-308). Since women can bear and care for only a relatively small number of offspring during the course of their lives, the theory posits that women will make more calculated mate choices, striving for a man who will provide for them and their children for the long haul. In particular, status and economic resources should arguably be more attractive to women for this reason. On the other hand, men can father an unlimited number of offspring without facing the costs of child-rearing. This makes it more advantageous for men to seek multiple partners who will guarantee their genetic continuation. What might appear like shallow attraction to physical characteristics such as a large bust or lavish blond hair is in fact responsiveness to cues of youthfulness and health—markers of reproductive success. Thus, from an evolutionary perspective, compared to women, men are hypothesized to be more driven by physical attractiveness.

Ample research has tested this hypothesis but found mixed support for it. In a statistical reevaluation of data from multiple studies conducted in the past, Feingold (1990, 1991) concluded that overall physical attractiveness matters more for men than for women. However, many studies have found that physique plays an equally pivotal role for both sexes (e.g., Asendorpf et al. 2011, 24; Luo and Zhang 2009, 950). Malakh-Pines (2005) combined in-depth interviews with survey data from samples of US American and Israeli men and women asking them to recall what attracted them when they first met their current romantic partner. Although appearance was cited more often by men than by women, physical attractiveness played an important role in overall attraction for both genders (216). In other words, even though men do rate physique as more important than women do, physical attractiveness is one of the top considerations for women as well (e.g., Pines 1998, 151).

Nor is there clear support for the assertion that a prospective mate's social and economic status would be of great importance for women but not for men (e.g., Asendorpf et al. 2011, 24 vs, Luo and Zhang 2009, 950). Moreover, it appears that there is a discrepancy between what people claim to be important in their mate choice and which factors guide people's actual preferences. Compared to men, women may rate earning potential as more important in evaluating a prospective partner; however, there are no gender differences in the effect of partner's economic status on people's actual relationship initiation (e.g., Eastwick and Finkel 2008, 253).

Some studies found that personality traits have little to do with mate preference (Luo and Zhang 2009, 950; Olderbak 2017, 56). The most frequently cited attraction factors were relational characteristics (sense of humor, caring, warmth) and intelligence (Malakh-Pines 2005; Regan et al. 2000).

Do PSRRs follow the same patterns? In our research of US adolescents (Tukachinsky and Dorros 2018), we posed an open-ended question asking what it was that made them fall for the media figure with whom they had a PSRR. Two coders then analyzed their responses and determined for each response whether it referred to appearance ("she is beautiful," "her smile," "his looks"), professional aspects (e.g., "his voice," "talented," "loved the lyrics"), or personality (e.g., "kicks butt," "fun," "smart"). Sixty-two comments referenced the appearance of the media figure, compared to only forty-four and forty-three comments concerning the media figure's work and character (respectively).

The emphasis on physique resonated in the closed-answer section of the survey as well. Survey participants were asked to what extent various qualities described the media figure they had a PSRR with in terms using a scale from 0 ("not at all") to 10 ("very much"). The top characteristics were physical attractiveness (9.22) and being fun and exciting (9.04), followed by having a sense of humor (8.95) and being sociable (8.85), sexy (8.77), intelligent (8.38), and caring (8.20). Interestingly, qualities that are often rated as the most desirable traits for a partner (and were in fact top-rated characteristics of an ideal partner in a sample of college students) were rated as relatively less characteristic of PSRR targets. They scored lower on loyalty and fidelity (7.81), shared interests (7.55), and shared values (7.44).

Not surprisingly, these responses correspond to what drew the adolescents' interest in the media figure to begin with. When asked what made them fall in love with or develop a crush on the media figure, they overwhelmingly (42.9%) cited the media figure's physique (e.g., "his looks," "how she looks, smiles," "she is beautiful and carries herself well"). Referencing the media figure's talent ("I liked how he acted on the show," "great singer") and references to the media figure's personality ("he was funny and charming and stood up for himself and what he believed in," "he is strong and sensitive") were much less frequent (25.4% and 23.8%, respectively). Another 7.9% of the reasons provided were global assessments ("his adorableness," "He's just such a perfect person in every way," "she is really cute").

Similar results emerged from a survey of the national sample of US adults. I presented the participants with the same open-ended question, and again, physique was overwhelmingly the most cited factor that drew the respondents' attraction to the media persona, mentioned by 55.8% of respondents, followed by character (22.3%) and talent (14.2%), and 7.8% referred to the target in general terms such as "cute" and "perfect." Both men and women cited physique as the reason for attraction to the PSRR target. However, interestingly, in this sample, men were in fact more likely to do so (66% of men vs. 46.4% of women mentioned physical attractiveness).

CONCLUSIONS

So what have we learned so far? By any metric used, PSRRs seem to be very commonplace. Unlike the popular notion and cultural representation of PSRRs, they are most certainly not restricted to adolescent girls. Rather, they seem to occur equally among both sexes. Although the most meaningful PSRRs do seem to date to adolescence and young adulthood, people continue to experience them across the lifespan throughout their lives.

The association between the propensity to have a PSRR and the respondents' current age is intriguing. Perhaps it hints at the possibility that there are some generational differences, although it is unclear whether the difference is in one's actual predisposition to have a PSRR or one's level of comfort reporting a PSRR in a survey. In other words, could it be that members of Generation X, Millennials, and Generation Z are more likely to develop PSRRs than Baby Boomers? Or is it that Baby Boomers have as many PSRRs but are more reluctant to disclose these experiences to others?

Surprisingly, contrary to common misconception, no gender differences have been observed in the prevalence or intensity of PSRRs. If men are as likely (or, perhaps, even more likely) than women to engage in PSRRs, why is the female adolescent fan stereotype so persistent? Are men less uncomfortable disclosing such experiences?

Physical attraction is a major factor driving PSRRs. This pattern of responses can be interpreted in a number of ways. First, the fact that physical attraction underlies PSRRs' initiation, rather than attraction to the traits that are valued as most important in serious relationships, may reflect and emphasize the hedonic value of the PSRR. Adolescents and adults across gender and age groups were attracted to media personalities first and foremost because of the media figure's to-be-looked-at-ness (to use Mulvey's term for the media's sexualizing gaze) and entertainment value—humor and excitement. Rather than engaging in PSRRs with figures who would be compatible partners in real life (e.g., based on shared values and interests) and that would ensure reciprocity (through trust and partnership), media audiences engaged in relationships that were free of these real-life constraints and were more playful and hypersexualized. This also explains why the physical component of PSRRs is rated so much higher than their emotional aspect. Clearly, at least for adolescents, sexual attraction is the driving force guiding PSRRs. These findings resonate with some of the earliest research on PSRRs. In Blumer's (1933) interviews with young adults and adolescents, sexual attraction to movie stars was highly prevalent. As one white, 16-year-old high school senior explained, "Whenever I look at these good-looking men on the screen, I just sigh! And wish he would take me in their arms and kiss me like they do those pretty women" (104). However, given how important physical attraction is in guiding romantic attraction, it can also be said that even though PSRR does not follow the *desired* characteristics in a mate, the *actual* patterns of developing romantic attraction are fairly similar both in reality and in mediated relationships.

Chapter 4

How Do I Love Thee?

Maintenance of Parasocial Romantic Relationships

From the time the relationship is initiated until it dissipates—for as long as the relationship exists—it has to be tended. To sustain the relationship, partners engage in a variety of relationship maintenance behaviors that encompass both routine actions that people perform habitually and more strategic, intentional efforts (Stafford 2003, 54–56). Routine maintenance entails day-to-day activities, including, for example, discussing one's day, doing one's share of household chores (Baxter and Simon 1993, 237), spending time with common friends, or watching together a favorite television show (Gomillion et al. 2016, 865–866). Another important form of maintenance is expressing intimacy and affection, both verbally (e.g., discussing one's inner thoughts and feelings, offering advice) and nonverbally (e.g., holding hands) (Baxter and Simon 1993, 237). More strategic behaviors entail, for example, romantic gestures (e.g., bringing flowers) and repair maintenance, such as talking out problems (237). In turn, engaging in these various behaviors has implications for the relationship satisfaction and stability (Stafford 2003, 71).

Communication lies at the core of all of these practices (Dindia 2003, 9–14; Stafford 2003, 58–59). As Kathry Dindia, one of the most prominent researchers in this area, states in her opening sentence of an overview of the field: "To maintain a relationship, partners must communicate with one another" (Dindia 2003, 1). Virtually all of these communicative behaviors—from routine self-disclosure to celebrating anniversaries—involve active engagement of both partners. How, then, do individuals maintain parasocial relationships (PSRs) that are, by definition, unidirectional?

As a matter of fact, interpersonal relationships too can go through times when partners are barred from interacting face to face or even via mediated channels. Interpersonal communication scholars have theorized how individuals engage in specific behaviors to ensure relational continuity during

35

such times of non-copresence, or interactional absence (Sigman 1991). Some of these behaviors occur prior to separation (in preparation for hiatus in face-to-face interactions) and after the separation (reuniting in person after being apart). However, of particular relevance to the parasocial context are the "introspective units"—behaviors that ensure relationship continuity *during* the physical and communicative separation (115). Specifically, introspective relational continuity units involve affiliation artifacts. These are physical objects that signify the relationship's existence and construct one's identity as part of that dyad. For example, individuals display photographs depicting their loved one, wear a wedding band, or use their absent partner's garment (116). Merolla (2010, 174–175) offered further nuance to this theorization, suggesting that relational continuity behaviors can occur on three levels. First, on an intrapersonal level, individuals think about their loved one, ruminating about the relationship, revisiting memories of the time they spent together, and holding imaginary interactions with them. On a dyadic level, individuals engage in mediated communication with their physically absent partner (e.g., write them a letter or call them). Finally, on a network level, individuals use their social connections to discuss the relationship and share stories and memories about their faraway partner.

Little is known about how PSRs in general and romantic PSRs in particular are maintained. The current chapter offers a first look at these strategies by examining data from surveys and interviews, combined with theories and research on how individuals manage nonmediated relationships, both face to face and in times of non-copresence.

PSRR MAINTENANCE BEHAVIORS

Shared Time

Spending time together is critical in facilitating friendships. Research has estimated that it takes about 30 hours of contact over the course of several weeks for an acquaintanceship to transform into a casual friendship (Hall 2019, 1287). It takes 140 hours of shared time to grow a "good friendship" (1287). In fact, the sheer amount of shared time is a unique contributor to friendship development, independent of other important maintenance behaviors (1289).

Applying these notions to PSRs, the equivalent to spending time together in a mediated context is exposure to the media figure. Thus, not surprisingly, consumption of media featuring the media-based romantic partner is a key component of PSRRs. All the interviewees stated that they watched and rewatched the films and TV shows starring their favorite actor or character, or listened excessively to the music artist's songs. Although the media user is a spectator, not an active participant in the events depicted in the media, they can experience them vicariously. By projecting themselves into the media reality, the interviewees felt that they were in fact sharing the media figure's world. By identifying with other characters starring opposite the love interest in the narrative, viewers were able to experience fictional events as if they were happening to themselves.

Moreover, for some, the media content serves as a springboard for imagining new scenarios about themselves and the media figure. For example, Alex (interview #20) shared that she regularly fantasizes about the fictional character she is in love with. In her daydreams, she is part of her beloved character's fictional universe. The plots she imagines are a spin-off from the actual media-based narrative. She described her fantasy plots:

> And then usually it will be like a happy ending story, and the challenges that [we] encounter are not like emotional things, but [. . .] because it's an action and fantasy genre it's more about, like, saving each other or something like that.

Similarly, Allegra (interview #24) recalled having "the characters play out stories in [her] own head" based off *Star Trek Voyager*. She imagined new narratives featuring herself as a local girl on a distant planet. Lieutenant Paris would meet her character on a mission, develop a crush on her, and "rescue her because she'd be in some sort of danger."

Other times, individuals reported imagining themselves sharing time and activities with the media figure in ways entirely divorced from the original media content. While in her earlier PSRRs Allegra (interview #24) imagined herself as a character situated within the fictional universe of her love interest, she later transitioned to plotting "realistic" scenarios of how her path could cross with the actor's in real life. For example, she fantasized about conceiving a romantic relationship with Jeremy Renner while working alongside him on a movie set. In another fantasy, after Renner's first son was born, Allegra imagined herself as the family's babysitter "hitting it off" with the new father.

One particularly common theme across these fantasies is serendipitously encountering each other. For example, Damian (interview #17) fantasized about running into his beloved singer in the airport, Jessica (interview #23) and Flora (interview #8) imagined bumping into their parasocial crushes at the mall or a local Starbucks and getting coffee together. In a national sample, 30.4% of the respondents who had a PSRR said they had frequently ("6" or "7" on a 7-point scale) imagined that their media love interest would pick them out of a crowd and see them as special.

Once the imaginary relationship is conceived, media users imagine engaging in shared romantic activities with their love interest. In a national survey, 33% of those who had a PSRR reported frequently imagining what it would be like to be in an actual relationship with their beloved media figure. Gilli (interview #1) recognized that what triggered these romantic ideations was when she found herself in situations with romantic potential. For instance, when "walking down the street and see[ing] a nice restaurant" she would imagine her beloved media figure with her and reenacting a romantic fantasy. Similarly, Allyssa (interview #10) fantasized about ice skating together with her celebrity crush, and Breanna (interview #7) recounted imagining herself and her parasocial love interest walking on the beach and spending Christmas together. Damian (interview #17) imagined going with his parasocial partner to a music store, singing together with her, or just talking to her about everyday things. Cindy (interview #3) described shared leisure activities and friends:

> [. . .] going to his favorite artists' concerts. He's also really good friends with Khalid and I love Khalid. So like meeting some of [his] friends would be really cool. And then also like, introducing him to all of my friends, even though we're all just like ordinary people. Like, I would definitely want, like, that level of relationship where we could meet each other's friends and it could not be "oh I'm meeting this famous person," it's just like meeting like, this person's friend.

Some media users, like Damian (interview #17) imagined what their day-to-day life would be like as a married couple. Others imagined relational milestones like engagements and weddings. Breanna (interview #7), for example, imagined a "really romantic" proposal with "a really big ring, because he's Justin Bieber" and having a beautiful beach wedding attended by many people.

FAN FICTION AND JOURNALING

The creation and consumption of fan fiction seem to be a powerful device for facilitating the imaginary processes underlying PSRRs. Skyler (interview #16) described the role of fan fiction writing in maintaining his PSRRs with a fictional character on the television series *Supernatural*:

> My fanfic journal was a place for me like to develop my relationship with Dean. So when I wrote fanfiction I not only was expressing my feelings, but [. . .] acting upon those feelings in experiencing my fantasies with Dean. Like, our relationship came to life when I wrote. It was like [. . .] I physically felt whatever I was writing about. It sounds cheesy but I can't think of any other way to explain it. [. . .] Basically, if I was writing about kissing Dean it was like I could

close my eyes and feel his lips against mine. It was the closest I could get to like physically being with him. It was like an intense craving being satisfied when I could read back what I wrote about my desires for Dean.

In a somewhat similar, although less intense way, Cathy (interview #19) used journaling to reflect on her feelings and process her emotions and thoughts concerning her parasocial love interest. Moreover, rereading her journals enabled her to revisit and relive these experiences later on: "When you write about it and then go back and read it, it brings you right back there."

Creating fan fiction is not very common, however. Only four of my interviewees admitted to writing fan fiction, and in a national sample, 59.1% stated that they had never created any form of fan art (short stories, drawings, etc.). Consumption of fan fiction seems to be much more common, although unfortunately, I did not ask about this practice on its own. Several of my interviewees reported reading fan fiction and finding it instrumental in generating their own relational fantasies. Brianna (interview #7) described her interest in "imaginaries" or "imagines"—romantic short stories, often told from a first-person perspective, describing the romantic relationship between a fan and a media figure (interview #7):

It's like when people make up stories about, um, a celebrity and like things that you would do with them, and a lot of them are really cute and they talk about, like, dates you would go on and stuff. [. . .] And then they [. . .] usually make them out to be nice people. Everything that you would like, want. Like on Valentine's Day, he bought you all these flowers and teddy bears and took you out on a romantic date. And so like, it's what you'd imagine.

Self-disclosure

From discussing mundane details of one's day to divulging deep and private thoughts and feelings, self-disclosure is critical for cultivating mutual understanding and fostering intimacy in interpersonal relationships (Greene, Derlega, and Mathews 2006). Furthermore, self-disclosure, joking, and expression of affection create a sense of belonging and affiliation in the relationship (Hall and Davis 2017). Notwithstanding talking to the media characters displayed onscreen when one is watching a movie or television show (e.g., Dibble and Rosaen 2011, 129), the fan's ability to engage in these behaviors directly in a parasocial context is limited to nonexistent. There are, however, a number of other proxies.

MEDIA CONTENT

Many media outlets offer opportunities for media figures to engage in self-disclosure. Some can be direct. For example, interviews with a celebrity involve the media figure in direct disclosure of personal information and engage the media user in a quasi-dialogue. More indirectly, learning about the celebrity's private life in gossip magazines, websites, and entertainment news serves the same purpose. Although this information is not sourced by the celebrity him- or herself, it makes the media user privy to the media figure's intimate life, which is, in part, what direct self-disclosure is about.

Indeed, thirsty for details about the lives of their beloved media figures, fans often engage in extensive research to learn about them. Of the 343 individuals who had a PSRR who participated in a national survey of adults that I conducted, only 16.3% said they never looked up information about their PSRR target in magazines, online sources, books, or other sources, while 39.9% said they do this very frequently ("6" or "7" on a 7-point scale). In the interviews, virtually all of the participants mentioned "researching" the media figure as an integral part of their relationship. As Damian (interview #17) explained: "Once you care about somebody and you want to be closer to that person you simply try to learn about them."

The most common subject they were interested in learning about was the media figure's actual romantic and family life. Although many admitted to feeling jealous seeing their loved one involved with someone else, they also appreciated this as a proxy for self-disclosure—an opportunity to see another aspect of that celebrity, enabling them to fancifully project themselves into that relationship and use the factual information as fodder for their own fantasies. For example, Ion (interview #2) described his motivation for researching the romantic life of the singer he was in love with:

> [. . .] it's fun to see her in a romantic relationship because then I can kind of see what she's like in that kind of setting, and imagine myself more in that setting [. . .] like pretend it's me in the photo. [. . .] you kind of get to see that side of her because you wouldn't be able to necessarily when she's not [featured in gossip magazines]—you don't get to see that.

SOCIAL MEDIA

Social media platforms offer the ultimate opportunity for the media figure to provide self-disclosure directly to their followers, while also at least theoretically enabling a direct interaction with the media figure. An analysis of media users' responses to celebrity Instagram posts suggests that followers are particularly fond of ostensibly "backstage" images that make them privy to the celebrity's personal and private, rather than professional, life (Tukachinsky et al. 2019, 175–177). This can apply to fictional characters as well. Media producers and fans maintain social media accounts impersonating fictional characters to allow others to interact with the fictional character, for example, by sending the fictional character birthday wishes or commenting on events that take place in the fictional narrative. Indeed, in a survey of adolescents aged 13–17, Bond (2016, 658) found that following a favorite media figure on social media was associated with stronger PSR regardless of whether the media personality was a fictional character or a real celebrity PSR.

Of course, reaching out to media personalities and trying to interact with them is not a new phenomenon, nor is it restricted to non-fictional targets. Back in the eighteenth century, for example, Jean-Jacques Rousseau was showered with fan mail, including many seductive letters from female reader admirers (Scott 2006, 327). One of them, Marie-Anne Alissan, had a lengthy correspondence with Rousseau in which they wrote each other in character, as Julie and Saint-Preux.

Somewhat surprisingly, my research found that following a media figure on social media or the celebrity's own website is a less common practice that only 27.4% of the survey participants reported engaging in frequently or very frequently. In part, this is an artifact of age. For example, Gina (interview #6), who is in her 30s and did not grow up with social media, uses Facebook to stay connected with extended family and long-distance friends, and for her the idea of connecting to celebrities is "creepy—like if I knew him on a personal basis." In the national sample, older individuals were generally less likely to use social media for connecting with media figures.

However, other ego-defensive psychological reasons may come into play as well. Several interviews specifically avoided following their beloved media personality, or restricted their online interactions in fear of losing control and escalating the relationship to what they would consider to be unhealthy levels. As Cindy (interview # 3) described:

> I haven't actually allowed myself to follow him on Snapchat because I feel [. . .] like it's stepping over the line. [. . .] I just think I would think about it too much and at that point, it would get unhealthy.

Even those who did follow celebrities did not try to use social media platforms to communicate with them. What seemed to hold them back was the conviction that their love would not be reciprocated. Specifically, my interviewees said they would not comment on their beloved media figure's social media because the media figure would not see it or respond to it, and because theirs would be just another comment buried in an endless stream of comments from other fans. As Alex (interview #20) explained:

> I would have to say that "I love you" or stuff like that, which is kind of like same things that a ton of other people are already commenting. [. . .] And like, adding one more, that's something I know they're not going to see. And it's like, can I do anything? I really just don't comment.

While they fantasize about being picked from a crowd and become someone special for the media figure, they realize that they are merely one more fan among an endless number of fans who post, send comments, and even attend meet-and-greet events. In other words, for my interviewees, reaching out to the celebrity was seen as a threat—a likely rejection shuttering the ideal image they painted in their fantasy. Kathrina (interview #9), for example, shared with me early in the interview her fantasy of becoming Justin Bieber's girlfriend:

> Maybe one day I would get to come to a show or a meet-and-greet and, like, somebody takes me backstage and he, like, looks at me and is, like, "Oh my God, you're the one." I mean, that's what every girl dreams of but like, "Oh my God, like, you want to fall in love" and like, "You're everything that I've looked for" kind of thing.

However, although she had the opportunity to attend a meet-and-greet event, she decided against it in order to protect herself from disappointment, knowing that the real meeting would not live up to her fantasy:

> I don't feel like I missed out because it's just one out of millions of a chance because there's so many girls, always, all around him. I think I would have felt more [. . .] upset inside and more heartbroken and more like I missed my chance [. . .] I just didn't want to be disappointed so I would rather keep it alive than just been bluntly denied to my face because I could never imagine—like the fantasies I had in my head like, I couldn't imagine going to an actual meet-and-greet and him being like, "Oh my God you're the one falling in love with me" he just [. . .] hugs me like every other fan and then I just walk away. So, I think that would have been the most disappointing and the most heartbreaking out of it all, so I guess I just didn't want to try.

In fact, this is very similar to what did happen to one of my interviewees. Peggy (interview #13) was indeed deeply disappointed upon meeting Justin Bieber in real life at a meet-and-greet event:

> He just stood there like a statue, [. . .] it was like taking a picture of the cardboard cutout. Like, he had glasses on. He had a hat on. He didn't say anything. He just stood there, [. . .] put his arms up, and [. . .] didn't smile, just like a statue. And

then you just walk away. And so it did not, like, live up to my middle school expectations. Obviously, the circumstances were different, and I was probably, you know, [was] the 10,000th person he had met that day.

It, therefore, seems adequate that many of my interviewees wanted to keep the relationship special by maintaining it entirely in the imaginary realms rather than being hurt by being yet another person in a crowd of fans or another comment buried on a busy social media feed—their love unrequited.

Conversely, Cathy (interview #19) and Sierra (interview #12), both women in their 50s, had attended numerous concerts and in-person events with the music artists they had a PSRR with. While acknowledging that they were probably an anonymous person in a crowd, they also felt like their devotion was rewarded. Sierra attended 217 concerts of her parasocial love interest and multiple meet-and-greet events. She recounted:

I know that we're [the fans are] just a bunch of, you know—I don't know whether he thinks we're just a bunch of crazy people, I have no idea! Because sometimes I know, like this last time I met—I had my meet-and-greet with him [. . .] as I approached him, he said, "Oh, hi" like he almost, you know, knew who I was or something.

She then ascertained the possibility that perhaps he recognized her face even if he did not know her by name because he had seen her so many times:

And I mean, I've been to 217 of his concerts! [. . .] and I always try to sit, you know, within the first 10 rows. [. . .] And so, it just kind of makes me laugh and go, "Oh, I don't think he recognizes me." Um, maybe he does.

Cathy too realized that she was one of many fans but nonetheless felt that she experienced even slight reciprocity and at least a momentary interpersonal connection. She told me about a book signing event she had attended. After a long drive and standing in an hours-long line

[. . .] they literally were like, you put the book down. He signs it. You move on. Don't talk to him. Don't try to take pictures with [him]. Nothing. Just get your book signed to move on. And we waited and I waited in this line. And when I got up to put my book down and I thought I was going to die. He's standing right in front of me. And he looked up at me and he said, "is this yours, love?" And, like, if I died at that moment my life would've been complete. He called me "love!"

Relational Artifacts

Displaying relational artifacts is a powerful way to symbolically celebrate a relationship and enhance feelings of positivity. This practice, however, is particularly important during times when partners are unable to interact with each other (Sigman 1991, 116). In times of separation, these relational artifacts—wearing a wedding band or displaying photographs of the loved one—serve an important function in declaring the existence of the relationship despite the hiatus in interaction, and they affirm a person's identity as a member of that relationship unit.

Indeed, as reported in other past research (Allen and Ingram 2015, 145–148), it was very common among interviewees to hang posters and create collages of pictures featuring their beloved media figures. Some put the media figure's picture as their phone or computer background image. When asked to describe what these practices mean to them, they talked about how seeing their loved one's face made them feel connected and enhanced their mood.

The fans related to their parasocial love objects through consumerism, such as by purchasing products the media figures endorsed (e.g., fragrance lines) or merchandise such as T-shirts. As Peggy (interview #13) reflected on her crush on Justin Bieber, "I had, like, I heart JB stuff everywhere." Such consumer behaviors fulfill multiple functions, both internal (e.g., establishing a symbolic connection with the media figure, fandom identity construction) and external (e.g., projecting their fan identity to the outside world). For example, Jennifer (interview #23) said she purchased a complete line of stationery items featuring images of Harry Styles, whom she was in love with at the time, because it made her feel good to see his face at all times, but also because it was her way of defining herself as a fan and sharing her parasocial passion with other fans.

Not only does the act of purchasing such items make fans feel connected to their beloved media figures, but they also see it as a way to "support" the celebrity. In turn, financial support has been deemed a symbol of their loyalty and a way of maintaining reciprocity in a relationship: "It just feels good to make something and support them," Gilli (interview #1) explained when discussing her investment in her favorite K-pop group's merchandise and her practice of spending hours drawing pictures of her beloved singer to re-create the band's official photographs.

Communication with Other Fans

The maintenance behaviors discussed thus far occur on the intrapersonal level (internal thought processes of reflecting on the relationship and handling imagined interactions) as well as on a dyadic level (attempting to interact with the media figure). Additionally, Merolla (2010, 175) suggests that individuals can use their social network to maintain relational continuity with an absent partner. By sharing memories and stories about their loved ones with friends, fans not only revisit their relational experiences but also affirm the relationship by identifying themselves in the eyes of others as a member of a dyad.

This practice is relevant to PSRR maintenance as well. To substitute for lack of direct communication with the parasocial love interest, individuals talk about the media figure with others, particularly with same-minded fans. Many interviewees mentioned that they sought out connections with others who shared their passion so that they could exchange pictures of the loved media figure and disclose their feelings. Some of my interviewees had a close friend or a small group of friends in their physical environment with whom they could share their fascination with the media figure; discuss the television show, movie, or music affiliated with the media figure; and exchange photographs and information they had learned about the media figure. Others felt misunderstood by people in their physical social circle but would find a tight-knit online community, joining fandom groups on social media or other internet platforms where they could share their passion. The need to narrow the discussion of the PSRR target to others who share these feelings is evident in Alex's (interview #20) story. In addition to her regular Instagram account, she created a private account that was shared with only a small subset of her regular social media connections. Only in this intimate circle did she feel comfortable posting photos of her PSRR partner and expressing her feelings about him. These fan-to-fan interactions create safe spaces to live the PSRR, creating an echo chamber that amplifies and affirms their feelings and relational identity.

Chapter 5

The Role of PSRRs in Adolescence

So far, we have established that many people spend tremendous energy and resources on their fantasy love objects. But why? What purpose do these imaginary relationships serve? This chapter offers two theoretical perspectives for understanding the role of PSRRs in adolescents' sexual and socio-emotional development: the compensation (also dubbed "substitution" or "social surrogacy") model and the preparation (or "simulation") model.

TWO MODELS OF PSRRS

The Compensation/Substitution Model

"My relationship with Michael is the best I have with anyone because I know he can't hurt me," divulged a 30-year-old Michael Jackson fan (Stever 2009). Alyssa (interview #10), whom I interviewed for this book, talked about her media crush in the same manner: "I think it's almost kind of like a safety thing. Because in the back of my head like I know that it's never going to happen so it's like, I'm not going to get hurt." Similarly, Allegra (interview #24), a self-described introvert, felt that "celebrities are safer [. . .] I don't have to, like, meet them in person. I don't have to, like, say something stupid because that's the biggest fear of an introvert." Both my interviewees and Stever's informant sought PSRs to satisfy their social needs without the risks associated with relationships with others in their actual social relationships.

For Ion (interview #2) too, a PSRR substituted in the absence of romantic opportunities:

I feel like naturally I have—in addition to sexual energy that everyone just kind of has to release—an emotional energy. Like I have to love someone and show someone that they are being appreciated, and when I don't have someone to do that to, I'll focus it on a fictional being.

Research on PSRs in general historically developed on the assumption that media characters serve as a substitution for relationship deficits in real life. Time and again researchers have argued that people are drawn to PSRs because these imaginary relationships satisfy their unfulfilled social needs. To test of the substitution hypothesis, scholars have searched for a correlation between levels of loneliness and PSR intensity, assuming that lonely individuals will make up for social denervation through imagined relationships (e.g., Rosaen and Dibble 2016; Rubin, Perse, and Powell 1985). However, to researchers' surprise, by and large, data across studies do not support this hypothesis (Tukachinsky, Walter, and Saucier 2020).

Following the same theoretical line of reasoning, researchers have considered various markers of poor social skills that would entice individuals to seek intimacy with media figures in lieu of relating to others in real life. However, again, for the most part, studies have failed to uncover a relationship between PSRs and barriers to forming social relationships, such as shyness (Ashe and McCutcheon 2001) and introversion (e.g., Levy 1979; Tsao 1996).

Attachment Style

One of the most studied presumed predictors of PSRs is *insecure attachment style* (Cohen, 1997; Rosaen and Dibble 2016; Rubin, et al. 1985). Attachment style refers to how people envision relationships with other people. It is a mental blueprint that guides individuals in relating to others. This mental model of relationships develops based on the person's early life experiences with a primary caregiver. Psychologists first documented variations in attachment style by observing how toddlers would react to their mothers leaving the room. Children with a "secure attachment style" exhibited a healthy reaction: They were upset when their mothers left but were happy to see them return, and after displaying affectionate gestures resumed independent play. On the other hand, those identified as having "insecure attachment styles" continued showing signs of distress even when their mothers were back. Some of these children clung on to their mothers in fear of losing them again. Others, to the contrary, tried to shield themselves from further rejection by ignoring their mothers and avoiding them upon their return, acting as if their disappearance did not matter. What these responses demonstrate is the different ways (or styles) in which children think about relationships based on their prior experiences with their mothers.

Children who were confident in their mothers' love knew that the relationship was a safe harbor they could always return to. Those who were ignored by their mothers or were treated in an inconsistent and unpredictable fashion were anxious about loss and rejection. As children grow up, these feelings are then generalized to other subsequent relationships, including romantic partners.

Communication researchers, therefore, have speculated that individuals who are more anxious about forming close relationships and those who avoid intimacy in real life will seek out PSRs as a safe alternative to "real" relationships. However, overall, studies have failed to find support for this hypothesis (Tukachinksy et al. 2020). Instead, they have discovered almost the opposite: the individuals who are most inclined to develop stronger bonds with others in their immediate environment are also the ones who are more likely to engage in deeper PSRs. Specifically, the most intense PSRs are usually experienced by both securely attached individuals who enjoy healthy intimacy in real life, and anxious individuals who are obsessed with not losing others. In conclusion, PSRs do not serve as a substitution for real relationships because of an inability to develop intimacy in real life, but rather they can be viewed as an extension of the same social skills and propensities. Those who enjoy intimacy with others in their lives seek intimacy with media figures as well. Those who cling to their romantic partners and friends are also obsessed with their favorite media personality. Conversely, individuals who avoid getting too close to others also do not cultivate intimacy in the mediated context.

PSRRs as Substitution in Adolescence

Although the compensation model has been largely debunked, there are specific conditions under which PSRRs are more likely to serve as a substitution for nonmediated relationships. For example, the work of Derrick, Gabriel, and Hugenberg (2009) points at the potential of short-term, situational social surrogacy effects, at times when individuals experience acute unfulfilled social needs. Experimentally arousing the need to belong by instructing people to ruminate on their relational struggles increased the amount of time these individuals then reflected on their favorite (but not other) television shows (357). In a correlational study more specifically looking at media characters, Greenwood and Long (2011, 289–290) found that a need to belong was positively associated with feeling intimacy with a media figure of the opposite sex, but only among single individuals. These findings suggest that it is not merely being single but the combination of being single *and* striving for an emotional connection with others that fosters attachment with a media figure.

Since PSRs are driven by a social motivation to form relationships, and considering the unique physiological and psychological developmental processes occurring in late childhood and adolescence, there is a reason to suspect that PSRRs could follow the compensation model in this particular age group. To understand the potential role of PSRRs in adolescence, it is important to first consider the biology of puberty. Many associate puberty with body hair growth, changes in boys' voices, and growth of breasts for girls. These processes are part of what is called *gonadarche*—the final maturation of testes and ovaries. This puberty stage occurs around age 9–10 in girls and a year or two later in boys. However, in actuality, puberty begins much earlier. The first phase of puberty, called *adrenarche*, starts around age 6–8 in both boys and girls. Adrenarche is not marked by external physical changes and can be precisely detected only with the use of a hormonal test. However, it is this early adrenal maturation that gives rise to sexual attraction and initial sexual desires, long before a child reaches fertility and undergoes development of secondary traits (Herdt and McClintock 2000).

In other words, children as young as 8 years of age can already experience initial sexual desire and sexual interest in others (Basson and Schultz 2007; Fortenberry 2013) even though they cannot act on it. This is where, arguably, PSRRs can fill in the gap and satisfy unfulfilled sexual urges in realms which do not involve physical maturation and/or readiness for carrying out an actual relationship. The gap between the early age of becoming motivated to engage in a romantic and sexual relationship and the time when this becomes appropriate is particularly wide for girls for three reasons.

First, as noted earlier, girls mature, on average, 2 years prior to boys. Thus, it has been suggested that many girls may feel ready for romantic experiences but realize that their male peers still lack the maturity to engage in such relationships (Karniol 2001, 61-62). Second, girls' emerging sexuality undergoes constant social scrutiny. Thus, girls may be concerned that if they start dating early they will be labeled as too promiscuous and could face social sanctions (Crawford and Popp 2003). Third, romantic relationships expose young individuals, particularly girls, to a variety of emotional and physical risks. Some girls might avoid involvement in romantic relationships in fear of being pressured to engage in sexual behaviors that they do not feel ready for. These concerns are not unwarranted. Research, indeed, shows that girls' early maturation coupled with being in a relationship with an older partner puts them at greater risk for a wide variety of risky behaviors, such as drug use, drinking, and paid sex (Halpern et al. 2006, 6). Other emotional risks of relationships are associated with rejection and breakup. Adolescents, regardless of their sex, are already in a fragile emotional state, while largely reliant on their peers for assurance, support, and sense of self. This makes this age group particularly vulnerable when relationships do not work out. As a result, involvement in a romantic relationship in the past 12 months and experiencing a romantic breakup constitute significant risk factors for a major depressive episode in adolescents (Joyner and Udry 2000; Monroe et al. 1999). The high emotional costs at stake makes it harder for adolescents to initiate a relationship. For example, young adolescent males often cite emotional restraints, such as shyness, as a major barrier to initiating a relationship with a love interest (Tuval-Mashiach et al. 2008, 479).

Taken together then, for girls in particular, dating early is either not an option (due to lack of suitable partners among their immature male peers) or dangerous (as it can damage their reputation or expose them to health and emotional risks). PSRRs offer a safe and effective alternative—an outlet for sexual and romantic urges that surface in puberty, fulfilling the adolescent's need to experience love and passion, sans the psychological and social repercussions that come with pursuing an actual dating relationship. In essence, PSRRs serve as a "placeholder" for subsequent "real" relationships until the opportunity for such relationships arises (Ward, Day, and Epstein 2006, 64). For example, Jennifer (interview #23), one of my interviewees, was homeschooled through middle school and attended an all-girls catholic high school. These schooling arrangements afforded her with few dating opportunities. Her romantic attachment to the actors starring in the *Supernatural* and *Sherlock* television series addressed her feelings of missing out on romantic relationships in real life and mitigated her self-doubts about ever being able to find her soulmate. Similarly, Gilli (interview #1) reflected on her fantasies about engaging in leisure activities for couples, like going on a carnival ride together, with her celebrity crush in lieu of an actual romantic partner:

> I've never had a boyfriend [. . .] It's kind of like placing [the celebrity crush] where I want someone else, because I can't really imagine myself with someone else that I've met. [The celebrity crush is] kind of like a placeholder in a way.

However, when the opportunity for a nonmediated relationship comes around, PSRRs outlive their purpose and dissolve. As Alyssa (interview #10) stated, her parasocial crush transpired because "I needed something, but when I'm in a relationship, I kind of have something." Interestingly, the reverse can happen as well. While the substitution hypothesis implies that individuals settle for PSRs as a substitution for actual dating, PSRRs can be so gratifying that they obviate the need for a real relationship altogether. In other words, PSRRs can be initiated as compensation for lack of actual relationships, but once they are established, the motivation to develop real relationships dissipates. For instance, Allegra (interview #24) recalled that in her teenage years she preferred media figures to the romantic candidates in her real life:

They're not a spy or a detective, or I mean, it's a 14-year-old boy. I mean, he's got nothing interesting going on other than going to school. So they just [. . .] paled in comparison to me because they didn't have an exciting backstory like the characters did.

However, she did not experience it as a deprivation:

I had no interest in dating, which probably was [because] my romantic energies were fulfilled by these crushes on these celebrities and these characters. And so I never really felt this need to form a relationship with a real person because those needs were being met through the media.

This dynamic explains why cross-sectional studies find no correlation between PSRs or PSRRs and a sense of loneliness or social deprivation. When bonding with media figures is examined at a single point in time, this lack of correlation merely affirms that PSRRs fully gratify media users' social needs. In other words, it could be that PSRRs are initiated as a substitution for lack of adequate social ties. However, because they are so effective at addressing these needs, lack of social relationships is no longer experienced as a deficit.

The Preparation/Simulation Model

Functional theories of daydreaming offer an alternative understanding of PSRRs. While historically, daydreaming was regarded as a maladaptive behavior, contemporary psychology has established daydreaming as a pervasive and healthy mental activity that is fundamental to people's well-being (McMillan, Kaufman, and Singer 2013, 626; Poerio and Smallwood 2016, 606). In fact, recently, neural psychologists have discovered that daydreaming is the "default" mode of the human brain (Andrews-Hanna 2012) that underlies planning, fosters creative problem-solving (McMillan et al. 2013, 626), and cultivates social-emotional skills (Immordino-Yang, Christodoulou, and Singh 2012, 357).

Young children love trying on their parents' clothes and shoes, and enjoy hours of pretend play, strolling, and feeding dolls. Through such games, children socialize into their future societal roles but also work out their current frustrations. Parents often smile when they overhear their children admonishing their dolls for the same kind of mischief in which the children themselves often engage. Sometimes, as part of a game, children will reenact their parents' actual responses to misbehavior, even using the exact same words to scold their dolls. Other times, children can develop alternative scripts and explore other ways to resolve a conflict. This is children's way of exploring their own feelings and desires and drafting possible scripts for future real-life situations that will call for such responses. As children grow up, daydreaming replaces overt play but serves the same function by allowing people to project themselves into various possible scenarios. These processes play such crucial developmental roles that researchers have warned that deficiencies in play (for children) and daydreaming (for adolescents) may pose a significant threat to their social-emotional and academic success (e.g., Immordino-Yang et al., 358). Because daydreaming is germane to PSRRs, it is important to consider how these functions apply to romantic socialization through PSRs.

PSRRs as Preparation/Simulation in Adolescence

From a constructive perspective on daydreaming, just as children explore social roles through pretend play, adolescents develop their romantic persona through fanciful romantic experimentation by imagining their ideal future relationships or fantasizing about being in a relationship with a particular person (Collins, Welsh, and Furman 2009; Larson, Clore, and Wood 1999; Tuval-Mashiach et al. 2008). Such fantasies crystalize the adolescents' relational expectations, develop their distinct perceptions of self in the romantic domain, and, for better or worse, enhance psychological readiness for future dating (Tuval-Mashiah et al. 2008).

PSRRs constitute an outlet for very elaborate romantic fantasies—a broad canvas for exploring, developing, and rehearsing romantic scripts and schemas that solidify one's romantic identity (Erickson, Harrison, and Dal Cin 2018). As such, PSRRs can be viewed as formative romantic experiences in early adolescence. They are, therefore, much more than a mere placeholder for actual relationships. Rather than serving as a bleak substitution for "the real thing," they are important and meaningful experiences in their own right that serve a critical developmental function in preparing and socializing adolescents for future dating relationships.

PSRRs as Self-discovery through Intracommunication

Social interactions offer an opportunity for expanding one's boundaries. By relating to others we can challenge ourselves and learn more about who we are. This is a process of self-expansion—an important function that drives much of human interaction. This notion has also been applied to media, demonstrating how immersion in fictional media worlds and the characters that populate them fulfill the same psychological needs as relationships with others (Johnson, Ewoldsen, and Slater 2015; Slater et al. 2014). Media consumers can playfully try on various alternative selves by borrowing other identities through identification with dissimilar characters and by vicariously experiencing situations and events that are outside the realm of possibilities in their real life (or that would have been unpleasant in reality but can be safely explored in one's imagination through media scripts).

Moreover, even nonmediated relationships with people in one's actual environment have some element of parasociability, as they too rely to an extent on imaginary interactions. As discussed in chapter 3, individuals rehearse their lines in dialogue and various scenarios of real-life interactions, both retrospectively (ruminating on an interaction that has already happened) and prospectively (imagining a future interaction) (Honeycutt 2014). Projecting oneself into these imaginary situations and acting out the interactions in one's imagination promote self-understanding and self-discovery. Moreover, practicing these scripts in one's imagination helps one solidify the script for future implementation in actual reality.

Not surprisingly, then, such imaginative activity, particularly when the content of the daydreams is positive, is associated with a variety of socially desirable outcomes. Individuals who have more positive social daydreams report greater relational satisfaction and love in their relationships (Mar, Mason, and Litvack 2012; Poerio et al. 2015). During life transitions, such as when entering college, positive social daydreams predict better adaptation to change and development of healthier social relationships (Poerio et al. 2016).

Accordingly, PSRRs can be viewed as another outlet for safe self-exploration activity. For example, the popular novelist Jodi Picoult reflected on her PSRR with Donny Osmond at the age of 6, saying it was a "perfectly safe relationship because it was completely one-sided." From her adult perspective, Picoult described her PSRR with Osmond as practice for adult relationships: "Role playing love is a dress rehearsal, a trial run before you give your heart to someone" (Alter and Singleton 2016, 4). A similar sentiment was expressed by young adult novel author Nicola Yoon, who had a crush on Michael Jackson at the age of 8 (21):

Boy bands and celebrity crushes are [. . .] safe spaces for girls to explore their feelings, their physical urges. These crushes are where we form our ideas of relationships and what we want from them and what we can contribute to them. I spent a year kissing Michael Jackson and found that I wanted a boy who was soft-spoken but not soft. A boy who would listen and hear all the things I had to say.

Similarly, some of the participants in my own interviews conveyed that the appeal of PSRRs lies in the freedom to imagine events any way they wish, having full control over the relationship. Since it is entirely in their imagination, a PSSR becomes a safe space for exploration. Cindy (Interview #3) called her PSRR "low risk" because:

it's more protective. You get to have more control over the narrative, where when like, [. . .] I feel like I don't exactly have to explain like exactly how I'm feeling. Um, and so like for me, I get to have control over the narrative.

Flora (interview #8) specifically described her PSRR as an opportunity to practice romantic scripts:

It's like a skill to work on. Like, even if it doesn't work out, like, it's okay because you [. . .] went through the steps. And, like, you know [that you can] adjust it for the next person.

Importantly, although adolescence is a critical time in the development of one's romantic and sexual scripts, the role of PSRRs as preparation through self-discovery is not strictly limited or unique to this age group, even if it plays a particularly prominent role for them. Individuals at any stage in their life may seek out PSRRs as a safe make-believe game that allows them to explore alternative realities and to shape, solidify, or challenge and reconsider their beliefs and expectations. As Mika (interview #11), a woman in her 40s, reflected on this role of PSRRs as a practice: "People need to practice feeling alive, like, feeling sexual and feeling desired and interested in the social world, in a way."

Putting the Models Together

The two views of PSRRs are not entirely divorced from each other but rather they can be seen as complementing. A person who strives to be romantically active but who cannot do so in fear of rejection or social sanctions can use PSRRs as a safe alternative to actual dating. While engaging in PSRRs out of necessity, the person also undergoes a process of self-discovery and self-expansion, growing more comfortable with and prepared for nonmediated relationships.

However, importantly, from a preparation model perspective, PSRRs do not *have* to replace romance in one's actual environment. PSRRs can be sought out not as a last resort—a pale substitution for the real thing—but because they are satisfying and engaging in their own right.

PSRRS ON THE ROMANTIC DEVELOPMENT TIMELINE

To better understand the role of PSRRs as substitution or preparation for dating relationships, my research attempted to map these experiences on the sexual history timeline, alongside other milestones in adolescents' romantic and sexual development. Figure 5.1 displays the results from three surveys using national samples of teenagers and adults and a sample of college students.

In an online survey we asked adolescents ages 13–17 when they started having sexual fantasies, when they had their first serious boyfriend or girlfriend, and the start and end times of their PSRR (if they had had multiple PSRRs, they were asked to choose the most important one). The data show that the average onset of the PSRR coincided with adolescents' first sexual fantasies as they turn 13 years old. Later that year (around the age of 13 years and 10 months) they tended to have their first boyfriend or girlfriend. However, the PSRR persisted through that time and did not dissipate until a year later, on the verge of their fifteenth birthday. Moreover, notably, the earliest meaningful media-figure crushes that adolescents reported dated back to the age of 6 or 7, which would correspond to adrenache — the first phase of puberty.

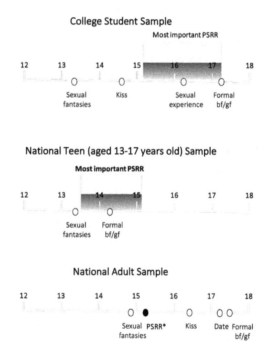

Notes:
* In the national adult sample, participants were asked about the timing of their first PSRR rather than the most intense or meaningful one. The national sample participants were not asked about the duration of their first PSRR.

Figure 5.1 Timing of PSRRs on the Sexual History Chart. Data from the College Student and Adolescent Samples Come from Tukachinsky and Dorros (2017). The Chart Represents the Average Age of Each Milestone. *Source:* Graphic created by author.

College student respondents reported that their most important PSRRs occurred later in life than the most important PSRRs reported by teenagers. This is perhaps because young adults had multiple PSRRs and in retrospect the earlier experiences were regarded as less important. In other words, the adolescent participants may not have yet experienced what they would come to see as their most important PSRR. It is interesting to see that college students report that their most intense and meaningful PSRRs arise at the same time as they began having sexual fantasies in general. It is impossible to tell which feeds into which. (Are the first sexual fantasies inspired by the PSRRs? Or do the PSRRs evolve in response to the sexual urges reflected by the sexual fantasies overall?) However, clearly PSRRs go hand in hand with overall sexual readiness, as adolescents become more interested in sexual experimentation, at least in the imaginative realms. Importantly, while the onsets of sexual fantasies and PSRRs are indistinguishable statistically speaking, there is a significant 7-month-long gap between the onset of sexual fantasies and PSRRs and one's first romantic relationship. This period can be interpreted either as substitution or as preparation. Either this is a time when the adolescent feels ready and eager to engage in a relationship but does not yet have a suitable partner (and thus engages in a PSRR instead), or it is a time of maturation, during which the adolescent gears up to become ready for acting on sexual fantasies. So which is it?

Arguably, the answer to this question lies in the timing of the PSRR dissipation. If a PSRR served merely as a placeholder, a fantasy alternative to unavailable real-life experiences, then one would expect the PSRR to disappear as soon as the adolescent found a suitable partner in a nonmediated world. However, this is not the case. A significant amount of time passes between beginning to date and outgrowing the PSRR. In other words, adolescents tend to maintain a PSRR while in a "real-life" relationship. This suggests that PSRRs offer something other than a placeholder for a future relationship. They do not substitute for a lack of relationships but respond to a need not satisfied by a boyfriend or girlfriend.

The data collected from a national sample of adults echoes these findings. While the specific ages when respondents, on average, hit each milestone were different from the ages in my survey of adolescents, a similar pattern emerged. The timing of all the events on the sex history chart were significantly different from each other, except the occurrence of the first PSRR and the first sexual fantasy, suggesting that both started around the same time. Only a year later, respondents begin to be sexually and romantically active — experiencing their first kiss, going on a first formal date, and having a first formal significant other.

To summarize, on average, the first PSRRs correspond to the onset of sexual fantasizing and they do not dissipate when the teen becomes romantically and sexually active. This suggests that PSRRs do not substitute for lack of opportunities to act on one's fantasy, but rather constitute just another component in the rich, fanciful romantic world that complements other romantic and sexual experiences. To further illustrate this point, participants in the national survey were asked directly whether they had been involved in a romantic relationship while they had their most recent or most memorable PSRR. Over half (53%) of the respondents said that the PSRR overlapped, at least in part, with having a romantic partner in their "real" life. Together, these findings suggest that although PSRRs can certainly serve as a substitution for at least some individuals, this is not the norm.

Chapter 6

The Effects of PSRRs on Romantic Beliefs and Dating

For the longest time, researchers across disciplines tended to dismiss the significance of adolescents' romantic experiences as a legitimate subject for scientific research. The scientific community deemed these fledgling relationships to be short-lived and inconsequential. Instead, they limited scientific inquiry to the "real," "grownup" relationships that lead to marriage and family building (Collins, Welsh, and Furman 2009, 632). Thus, adolescent romance (let alone fanciful relationships) has been gravely understudied and poorly understood. Only recently have scholars begun to realize that early romantic experiences do merit close consideration.

The human brain is constantly rewired in response to our ongoing experiences and the ever-changing environment. Relationships almost literally scar our brains, leaving a mark that influences on how we respond to the world in the future. Early social experiences are particularly important in setting the tone for future ones. This is why our bonds with parents or primary caregivers have a long-lasting effect on how individuals view relationships and their ability to experience emotional intimacy with others. Similarly, early romantic experiences must then play a critical role in shaping youths' romantic paths (Collins 2003, 16–18; Collins, Welsh, and Furman 2009, 642). Building on this notion, it is argued that in addition to actual dating experiences, imaginary, parasocial romantic experiences play a similar, critical role in psychological romantic development. In other words, if in adolescence having parasocial romantic relationships (PSRRs) is to dating what playing "family" is to assembling a real family for preschoolers, what then are the lessons that adolescents learn and internalize through these experiences?

MEDIA EFFECT ON ROMANTIC BELIEFS

Ask an 8-year-old to imagine a romantic date. What would it look like?

"A fancy restaurant with candles on the table and champagne, dim lights. [. . .] It's a French restaurant," said a fourth-grade African American girl. "At an Italian restaurant [. . .] and the lights are dim, and there are lots of candles around," echoed a fourth-grade white boy. Both children were participants in Bachen and Illouz's (1996, 298) study. One after another, children who had not ever gone on a romantic date recited the same exact fantasy, complete with a dinner in an expensive restaurant, offering sophisticated cuisine, accompanied by fine wines and candlelight (299). These children's fantasies converge into a unified narrative of what a perfect date should look like, how romantic partners behave, what being in love looks like to an outside observer, and what it feels like to those involved in the relationship. Where do these detailed images and scripts come from, provided that children lack firsthand dating experiences? How can they be so synchronized across children from diverse social backgrounds?

Like other cultural scripts, romantic scripts too are culturally transmitted, predominantly through media (Illouz, 1997)—from children's Disney movies to vacation advertisements to comedies, and even romantic subplots in action movies. Media portrayals of romance can be criticized for being unrealistic and propagating idealized and naive views of love. Most media narratives follow the three-act formula: a boy meets a girl, they lose each other, and they overcome enormous obstacles to reconnect. The variations are minor. Sometimes a boy meets a boy, or a girl meets a girl. In a dramatic genre, unlike a romantic comedy, the two may tragically fail to reunite, but the belief in the power (and merit) of love nonetheless serves as the underpinning of the narrative arch. This archetypical romantic formula runs through the Western culture from Orpheus in Greek mythology to contemporary blockbuster teen movies, and it exploits the same trope we may deem cliché.

First comes the "meet cute"—a serendipitous encounter between star-crossed lovers. They bump into each other, their belongings spill on the floor, and they bond over an awkward conversation while crawling on the floor to pick up their items. Meet cutes embody the myth of love at first sight and the existence of a unique soulmate just waiting to bump into you. Then, a cascade of disasters is unleashed, threatening the relationship—from Romeo and Juliet's parental disapproval to the threat of exposure as an imposter in *There's Something About Mary*. The lovers are on course to a tragic separation. Sometimes the obstacle is not an external force, but an initial dislike that the characters experience in their first encounter, when they find themselves stuck with each other. Forced to collaborate, they discover that opposites (or adversaries) actually attract and can in fact be each other's soulmates (*Addicted to Love, The Proposal*). Either way, the lovers work to overcome the obstacles, which are sometimes grotesque and unrealistic, and at times poignantly life-like. But love conquers all. Or at least the protagonists hope so, putting this goal above all because soulmates are forever, or at least they should be. Sure, some stories do not end with the lovers living together happily ever after. Sometimes they split. More often, the script writers separate them by death (*A Star Is Born, Me Before You*). But even so, the emotional journey on which the movie takes the viewer is enjoyable because it offers the audience an opportunity to appreciate love and humanity and enables them to ponder hefty philosophical questions (Bartsch and Oliver 2016): Can love be the answer to life challenges? (yes); Is life without love worth living? (no); Does loving someone mean letting them go? (All of the above: yes — because love means to sacrifice oneself, and no — because love conquers all). From children's movies (Hefner et al., 2017; Martin and Kazyak 2009) to soap operas, TV dramas (Kretz 2019), romantic comedies, and romantic subplots of non-romantic genres such as thrillers and science fiction films (Hefner 2011, 113), the formulaic narrative follows the same idealized romantic blueprint.

Not surprisingly, then, numerous studies have found an association between exposure to romantic genres and upholding idealized romantic beliefs. Most of these studies are correlational surveys, meaning they show only that heavy consumers of romantic media content also uphold stronger romantic beliefs (e.g., Hefner and Wilson 2013; Galloway, Engstrom, and Emmers-Sommer 2015; Kretz 2019). Of course, such studies cannot definitively conclude that watching romantic comedies *causes* more idealized romantic beliefs. The relationship is likely to work both ways—not only does romantic media content promote romantic beliefs, but also initial romantic inclinations are expressed as a preference for romantically themed media. Those who are cynical about romance probably do not enjoy romantically themed media, so they avoid watching it in the first place. But some experiments (Driesmans, Vandenbosch, and Eggermont 2016) also point to the fact that even short-term exposure to romantically themed media heightens one's romantic beliefs.

These studies, however, have considered exposure specifically to romantic stories that the viewer has passively observed and absorbed the message of. The young children in Bachen and Illouz's (1996) study showed that they were quick to learn romantic scripts from the media. Clearly, popular media romantic narratives socialize viewers form a young age to view romance in a certain way. However, PSRRs offer much more than the opportunity to observe media romances and gather information about romantic norms. As is outlined in the following section, the effects of observational learning notwithstanding, PSRRs offer a unique mechanism for affecting romantic beliefs and experiences in future romantic relationships.

THE EFFECTS OF PSRRS

Unlike learning through observation, engagement in PSRRs is an active process that involves trying out romantic scripts. Media users are not mere spectators of the scripts but are playing them out in their imagination through a meaningful relationship with a media figure. Moreover, the target of the PSRR does not have to be depicted in a romantic message in the first place. For example, many adolescent girls profess their love for Dr. House, the leading character in the hospital drama *House, M.D.*, a show that, though it does contain romantic subplots, is by no means a romantic genre per se (Tukachinsky 2011, 75). The romantic content that socializes the media user is not constructed by the scriptwriters or even by the media figure, but is a fruit of the viewer's own imagination.

Given that this romantic socialization is not a product of media content but is produced by media-user-generated scripts, will PSRR lead to more realistic romantic views? Do these imaginary romantic experiences prepare adolescents for healthier and better romantic relationships? The following section presents two opposite schools of thought that guided our theorization.

Competing Predictions

On the one hand, when media users lack an unrealistic romantic formula, they are free to ascertain more appropriate romantic scripts. Moreover, we know that social daydreaming is adaptive in general, fostering healthier and more fulfilling social relationships (e.g., Immordino-Yang et al. 2012, 357; Poerio and Smallwood 2016, 606). In fact, research on social daydreaming suggests that idealized fanciful relationships are not necessarily a bad thing, since it is positive imaginary social interactions in particular that have beneficial effects on people's actual social experiences (e.g., Poerio et al., 2015, 8–9).

On the other hand, there are reasons to believe that PSRRs have negative consequences. First, they are directed toward someone with whom no relationship can materialize, and such inherently unrequited love can be frustrating. Indeed, Mar, Mason, and Litvack (2012, 405–406) found that social daydreaming is only instrumental when it involves individuals from one's actual social circle, such as friends and family members. Fantasizing about people one cannot be in an actual relationship with, including fictional characters and romantic exes, is associated with negative feelings, such as loneliness and lower life satisfaction (405–406).

Second, since the relationship is imaginary, it is free to be unrealistic and foster unattainable standards, resulting in disappointment when real-life relationships cannot rise to that standard. This is especially likely to happen, we reasoned, because adolescents do not have as many realistic models from which to develop a blueprint for their romantic ideations. This is particularly true because even if the media figure does not appear in a romantic genre, the media context in which the viewer encounters that personality is nonetheless saturated with romantic ideals that are likely to promote unrealistic parasocial romantic ideations. Yet, given that PSRRs are not reenacted in the real world, the imaginary scripts never clash with the realities of actual relationships. Under these conditions, a person with a PSRR is free to create and mentally inhabit an entirely unrealistic fantasy that would lead to dire consequences if enacted in real life. What happens then when these unrealistic scripts are applied to real life? Will they set up the media viewer for disappointment?

Consider, for example, the predicament that Miss A shares in a letter published in Ann Landers's advice column in the *Chicago Sun-Times* (Horton and Wohl 1956, 227):

> It has taken me two weeks to get the nerve to write this letter. I have fallen head over heels in love with a local television star. We've never met and I've seen him only on the TV screen and in a play. This is not a 16-year-old infatuation, for I am 23, a college graduate and I know the score. For the last two months I have stopped dating because all men seem childish by comparison. Nothing interests me. I can't sleep and my modeling job bores me. Please give me some advice.

Ms. Landers responded bluntly to Miss A, reminding her that the persona she was in love with did not actually exist in reality but was a projection of a media-constructed personality (227):

> I don't know what you learned in college, but you are flunking the course of common sense. You have fallen for a piece of celluloid as unreal as a picture on the wall. The personality you are goofy about on the TV screen is a hoked-up character, and any similarity between him and the real man is purely miraculous.

Most likely, Landers's response did not convey anything that Miss A did not know already. As an educated young adult she probably realized that the target of her romantic feelings is "unreal." Yet, his perfect image overshadowed actual possible romantic partners that Miss A rejected upon comparing them to the media figure. In a similar vein, in the early 2000s, a 32-year-old woman posted an online article professing love to the fictional character MacGyver (Davis, n.d.). She attributed her inability to find a suitable partner to the fact that no real man could live up to the ideal standards her parasocial romantic partner had set. She concluded the post by stating:

Reruns of *MacGyver* on TV Land should really come with this disclaimer: [. . .]
Ain't no man on Earth actually like MacGyver. He is the untouchable male ideal
that every woman drools over, searches for, and then finally gives up on to settle
for someone who doesn't annoy the shit out of her too damn often. We apologize
if this character gives you false hope about your love life and its potential future.
Forgive us.

Both of these stories, while extreme, demonstrate how PSRRs cultivate
unrealistic romantic expectations that potentially lead to disappointment
when these unrealistic standards cannot be met in real-life romantic relationships. Such concerns about PSRRs' potential to threaten the social-emotional
well-being of individuals and even endanger normative social structure were
also raised in the context of pinup girl culture, when soldiers were returning
home to real girlfriends and wives after spending many months in PSRRs
with actresses.

Kiser (2013, 63) claims that it would be "nonsensical" for soldiers' romantic partners to feel threatened by pinup girls; a soldier "may have held dreams
of holding hands with a famous starlet then she visited the troops, but his
dreams, such as the dreams of the worrisome girl, were entirely absurd." The
author claims that "falling in love with a pin-up girl only happened when the
mind entered a state of juvenile fancy" (65). Pinup girls were created not as
ideal brides but for getting morale up as "objects of lust capable of spurring
the troops towards victory" (66).

However, why assume that both these outcomes (increased morale and cultivation of unrealistic romantic ideals) cannot take place? Even if unintended,
unrealistic romantic fantasies could potentially lead to adverse consequences
in real life. Indeed, during World War II, some raised concerned that returning soldiers would be affected by this fantasy. Kiser (2013, 64) reports that
the columnist Dorothy Dix was concerned that:

G.I.'s have lost their realistic snapshot of things and people as they see them
only through the rosy picture their fantasies paint. Thus, every man's wife or
girl he left behind becomes as pulchritudinous as the pin-up girls upon whom
he daily feasts his eyes and who establish his ideal of what a woman should
really look like.

And so, while veterans like Ernie Pyle reassured women that "personally
I don't see there's much conflict. I've never heard of a soldier writing to
his real girl to break off the engagement because he had fallen in love with
a picture" (Kiser 2013, 65), the *Oakland Tribune* reported a story about a
soldier—Private Webster—who divorced his wife because of pinup girls.
According to the wife's testimony, her husband constantly belittled her for

not measuring up to the looks of Betty Grable, specifically the pinup girl's eyes and blond hair (116–7).

Research Results

To investigate more rigorously and systematically the potential effects of PSRRs on youths' unrealistic perceptions of romance and subsequent romantic partners, Dr. Sam Dorros and I (Tukachinsky and Dorros 2018) conducted two surveys using a sample of US adolescents in a retrospective survey of college students, asking them to reflect on their teenage years. First, we, hypothesized that PSRRs would cultivate more idealized, unrealistic romantic beliefs. In turn, we asserted that these idealized romantic beliefs would lead to lower satisfaction with one's current romantic partner. Past research has identified five specific romantic ideals, including the beliefs that everyone has one special soulmate and that love conquers all. We did not ask about beliefs about love at first sight, which represent a script of initiation of relationships, but rather decided to focus solely on beliefs concerning relationship maintenance: "Love conquers all" and the expectation to love every aspect of the true soulmate.

We found that once we took into account adolescents' demographic characteristics (e.g., gender, age, ethnicity), intensity of physical PSRRs had no effect on their endorsement of idealized romantic views. However, regardless of a participant's background, the more intense the emotional PSRR they had with a media figure, the more they subscribed to unrealistic romantic ideals. Unfortunately, because only a few adolescents in this sample had a romantic relationship during the time of the study, it was not feasible to examine the effects of their PSRRs on their actual dating satisfaction. Instead, we attempted to ascertain this relationship over time in a retrospective sample of college students.

To this end, we surveyed college students and asked them to reflect on the PSRRs they had had growing up as well as to tell us about their current romantic partners and satisfaction in their romantic relationships. Once again, we found that physical PSRRs had no consequences for romantic beliefs or perceptions of nonmediated relationships. However, just as in the national sample of teens, emotional PSRRs were positively associated with idealized romantic beliefs. In other words, the college students who reported having the most intense emotional PSRRs in their adolescence had also had the most idealized romantic beliefs in their young adulthood.

Next, we asked those who were involved in a romantic relationship at the time of the study to reflect on how satisfying that relationship was. We also asked them about their perceptions of their current partner, requesting that they rate the partner in terms of various characteristics such as loyalty, generosity, emotional expressiveness, and prioritizing the relationship. As expected, we found that the intensity of the emotional PSRR in adolescence was associated with *lower* relationship satisfaction and a *less* favorable perception of the participant's current romantic partner. However, interestingly, this effect was independent of idealized romantic beliefs. In other words, PSRRs seem to impact relationship experiences directly, not as a function of distorted ideals.

A similar approach was employed by Erickson and Dal Cin (2017), who specifically studied female college students' current romantic selves in relation to their PSRR experiences recalled from the age of 12 to 14. An analysis of survey data from 376 young adult women showed that the intensity of the parasocial romantic attachment the participants reported having in their adolescence was a significant predictor of their current passionate romantic style. Moreover, intensity of PSRRs was positively associated with various maladaptive beliefs. First, PSRRs in adolescence were linked to endorsement of traditional gender roles within the romantic script, such as the belief that women should do whatever is necessary to attract a partner and acceptance of sexual double standards that excuse a lower relational commitment from men. Second, to the extent that the women had stronger PSRRs, their self-esteem was more heavily dependent on their relational status. These women put the well-being of their partners and the value of being coupled at all costs over their personal psychological well-being. Finally, although PSRRs were not directly related to sexual and romantic satisfaction in this sample, the researchers noted that stronger PSRRs in adolescence were predictive of a more negative appraisal of one's sexual experiences, as participants who had nurtured stronger PSRRs reported feeling more embarrassed, ashamed, regretful, and anxious when thinking about their sexual experiences.

The findings from both Erickson and Dal Cin's survey and my studies with Dorros are consistent with the theorization of PSRRs as a process of developing romantic scripts that ultimately are utilized in subsequent dating prelateships, but due to their unrealistic nature lead to maladaptive relational outcomes. Of course, the correlational nature of these studies does not allow for definitively establishing the direction of causality, but in-depth interviews with media users can offer insight into how PSRRs mold individuals' future relational experiences.

Idealized Romantic Scripts in Action: In Their Own Words

To gain a better understanding of the PSRR experience from the perspectives of people engaged in such relationships, I have conducted in-depth interviews that offer a unique insight into the content of the PSRR fantasy and individuals' self-conceived notions of the media's effects on them. My informants often mentioned that they enjoyed their power to create whatever world they wanted in their imagination. The narratives of their fantasy are specifically idealized and positive. As Breanna (interview #7) explained:

> You can [. . .] change things to your liking. Like if something's not going right, you can just be like never mind, like I want to change that. But in real life, you can't control other people's actions, you just have to go with what they give you.

My informants generally described their PSRRs as obstacle-free. The overarching theme in their fantasies was being pursued by the media figure. The interviewees reported that they typically imagined the media figure as the one to initiate the relationship, and sometimes they even had to overcome their initial reluctance or hesitation. Many fantasies revolved around the media figure's display of small or grand romantic gestures—from leaving small but thoughtful gifts and amorous notes to orchestrating surprise romantic trips. However, for the most part, the PSRRs were imagined as simply enjoying each other's company while engaging in a variety of leisure and mundane activities (as described in chapter 4). Together, these fantasies painted a very idealized version of ever harmonious, highly enjoyable relationships in which the media user served as a constant target of their partner's attention.

In fact, some interviewees made an explicit choice to edit out of their fantasies any negative aspects of romantic relationships. For example, Brianna (interview #7) specifically avoided reading imagines fanfiction that dealt with relational distress after she read a story in which Justin Bieber was cheating on the reader's character. "It was terrible," she described the experience of reading the story that forced her to engage in negative imaginative activity: "You just start crying and you're an emotional wreck." When informants did imagine relational challenges, such as an attempted return by the media figure's ex or a quarrel about the musician's frequent travel for their career, love always prevailed. "Sometimes I would imagine [problems] but then our love was so strong that we would totally get over them," summarized Jennifer (interview #23). The challenge to the romantic relationship was only presented as a dramatic climax that ultimately reaffirmed the media user's romantic ideals.

Not only was the relationship imagined to be perfect but the target of the PSRR was also idealized despite the informants being aware of the fact that this was unlikely to be true.

Gilli (interview #1) described herself imagining a "boyfriend with no flaws," Alex (interview #20) felt that the character she was in love with was "above all the other people," and Ion (interview #2) said about his media-based love object that "she can do no wrong." Similarly, Damian (interview

#17) said, "To me she is perfect, there is nothing I can think of that isn't perfect about her, I know this is probably not true, but for me she is perfect."

It is not surprising, then, that the survey results show that PSRRs that involve such idealized images set unobtainable relationship standards that can lower satisfaction in real dating relationships and result in a less favorable view of one's current romantic partner. When I asked the interviewees if they felt that PSRRs had such an effect on them, some maintained that they were not affected by their PSRRs, knowing they were fictional. For example, Cindy (interview #3) said that she "wouldn't want to base any actual relationship off my idealized [PSRR], because when you just imagine something, you can completely idealize it and make it perfect in your mind." However, some respondents did believe that their PSRRs had a lasting effect on them: "Because I developed those crushes when I was a kid and they imprinted on me or like into that" (Hunter, interview #13).

Gina (interview #6), for example, believed that falling in love with the male lead in the romantic drama *The Notebook* shaped her expectations from her real-life romantic partners: "I definitely knew I wanted somebody who was willing to wait for me, who loved me and was dedicated."

Katherina (interview #9) had a long list of desired partner qualities that she derived from her PSRR with Justin Bieber and looked for in prospective real-life partners. She sought a combination of hardness and softness, someone who would find her hard to get:

He serenaded the girls. I realized that like, I want to be serenaded like that. [. . .] It taught me that a guy *should* [emphasis in the original] want you that bad and he should feel about you like that and he should show it and if he doesn't show it, then he's not good enough. Like, he's not the right person because he doesn't like you that much.

It's still something I look for. To this day, that's like exactly what I want. I want somebody who can beat up 20 guys but then at the end of the day come home and hug me and kiss me and tell me everything's okay and kind of like, be gentle and like strong but like, nice at the same time.

In this process, Katherina had to eliminate many suitors:

I turned down everybody, I guess, because I was like, it's not good enough. Because I had—like I mean he's [. . .] a really good role model in what to look for so of course [. . .] nobody was ever good enough. But yeah, now I found a boyfriend that kind of looks like him, so yeah. And I've had a lot of guys who were like this and I've pushed all of them away you know, because [. . .] there are these standards were set when I was younger and growing up as a teenager.

Where like this is how a girl should be treated and this is how much a guy should like her.

Ultimately, realizing that their objects of parasocial love are nonviable targets, individuals settle for real-life partners even if they do not live up to the parasocial ideal. Cathy (interview #19), who is now in her 50s, reflected on a parasocial teenage crush that was recently rekindled:

If you said to me, you need to fly right now, [. . .] Bruce Dickinson wants to see you in England, I would be at the airport in 20 minutes. No doubt. No doubt in my mind. [. . .] I've even joked with my fiancé, say when I was going for the book signing, I was like, listen, just so you know, if Bruce Dickinson instantly falls in love with me, I will not be back.

Moreover, for some individuals, unrealistic romantic scripts in their imaginary relationships bled into their actual dating relationships. For example, Mimi (interview #22) recounted testing her high school boyfriend to prove that he was her true soulmate. Reenacting romantic scenarios that she had developed through her imaginary relationship with Harry Potter characters in fanfiction stories she wrote, Mimi broke up with her boyfriend to see if he would fight to win her back: "I knew that [. . .] I was going to have a happy ending, I was always going to be with him. I was always going to go back to him." At first, she said, "It felt good." However, she was ultimately hurt and devastated, as the idealistic romantic fantasy of a happy ending and love concurring did not unfold in reality as she had expected:

And then in my head after that we were going to stop fighting, which, of course, didn't happen. But in my head, I was like, OK, he came back, [. . .] that means that we're meant to be. Now everything's going to be perfect. And then when it didn't work, that was really hard. I guess that I was like, okay, maybe that was just [. . .] the first obstacle. And now, now here's the real climax. But the fighting kept happening and they [expectations of a happy ending] kept having to readjust. And in the end, the real climax was just us breaking up.

At 21, Mimi reflected on these teenage experiences and admitted that it was unhealthy to let her imaginary relationships drive her real relationships. Yet she still hoped to obtain the ideals she recognized as unrealistic. Reflecting on the underlying themes of her imaginary relationships, Mimi said she wished she were "able to have conflict and then come back and just know that everything's going to be OK at the end."

FINAL REMARKS

Taken together then, PSRRs are idealistic. They idealize the parasocial romantic partner and the relationship itself. However, intriguingly, for the most part, individuals do not see it as a problematic practice. In fact, they see the power to generate perfect scenarios as the main appeal of PSRRs and as a way to celebrate their power: "Nobody can say anything." Because the relationship is in their head—no one can judge, criticize, or challenge the idealized script they form in their imagination. They have the power to come up with the narrative.

Many of them do not recognize the potential for a PSRR to sabotage their actual relationships because they believe in a separation between the two (Cindy, interview #3), or because they do not admit that such high standards are unrealistic (Katherina, interview #9). Even those who did admit to the potential effects did not discuss their PSRRs in a negative way. This pattern of results reflects the long-standing dynamic of moral panic, wherein researchers, media, and mental health practitioners warn against media users' practices while fans claim ownership and agency in the process.

Chapter 7

Same-Sex PSRRs

For lesbian, gay, and bisexual (LGB) people, the mainstream media harbor the potential to be both pernicious and inspiring. On the one hand, historically, popular media have been the cornerstone of a heteronormative culture that oppressed those who did not conform to mainstream sexual dogmas. Although today same-sex relationships are commonplace in the mainstream media landscape (Bond, Miller, and Aubry 2019), for decades representations of LGBs were scarce (Mulligan 2018, 26–27). When sexual minority characters started appearing onscreen, they were often ridiculed and presented in ways that reinforced negative stereotypes (e.g., Fisher et al., 2007; Fouts and Inch 2005; Raley and Lucas 2006). Such limited and stereotyped portrayals of LGB individuals not only contribute to negative attitudes toward LGBs held by heterosexual audiences (e.g., Nisbet and Myers 2012) but can also have an insidious effect on LGB youth's self-perceptions and emotional well-being (Bond 2016b, 425; Bond and Miller 2017, 104). Moreover, media constitute a rich source of material for heterosexual script development, but there is a dearth of information for those seeking non-heteronormative scripts (Patterson, Ward, and Brown 2013, 181), which potentially leaves LGB youth underprepared for building same-sex relationships.

On the other hand, media also hold a massive potential to do the exact opposite. By offering positive, relatable, diverse, popular LGB characters, mainstream media both improve tolerance toward sexual minorities among heterosexual viewers (e.g., Bond 2020; Ortiz and Harwood 2007) and promote the psychological well-being of LGB media users (Bond and Miller 2017, 104). Specifically, media validate LGB adolescents' identity, reassure them that they are not alone, and provide them with role models and sources of inspiration and empowerment (e.g., Bond 2018; Bond and Miller 2017; Gomillion and Giuliano 2011). Moreover, media fill in the void left by school, families, and other community players, providing LGB youth with information about gay life, assisting LGB media users to consolidate their sexual identity and to come out to self and others (Bond, Hefner and Drogos 2009). Hence, as much as media serve as an important source of sex-related information for all adolescents, in the absence of other sources of information about same-sex relationships media play a particularly crucial role in the sexual socialization of LGB youth. Heterosexual teenagers rate family and friends as the most important sources of information on issues such as school, substance use, romance, sex, and family issues, whereas LGB teenagers list media figures as the second most important source of guidance and information on all these topics (after friends) (Bond 2018, 472).

Moving beyond media as a purveyor of information and a source of LGB role models, super-peers, and mentors, media can also serve as a substitution or preparation for actual relationships through PSRs (as discussed in chapter 5). In his examination of the place of PSRs in the lives of heterosexual and LGB adolescents, Bond (2018) found that LGBs were more likely than heterosexual teens to form PSRs with LGB media figures (471). This tendency was particularly pronounced among LGB teenagers who did not have LGB friends in their immediate social circles (471). These individuals also reported much stronger PSRs than heterosexual teenagers. Notably, while there was no association between heterosexual teenagers' PSR intensity and how lonely they felt (in line with the debunking of the substitution hypothesis) loneliness *was* positively correlated with PSRs among LGB teens (470). Moreover, LGB adolescents were particularly keen on forming PSRs with LGB media figures (470). These findings allude to the particularly meaningful role that PSRs can play in the unique circumstances LGB youth face. While past research has focused mostly on exposure to LGB-themed media and overall interest in and PSRs with media figures, this chapter specifically examines same- and opposite-sex PSRRs with media figures, situating PSRRs in the broader context of LGB child development and experiences.

THE ROLE OF PSRRS IN SEXUAL
IDENTITY DEVELOPMENT

There is no single path leading to identifying oneself as gay/lesbian/bisexual, reaching self-acceptance, and coming out to others (e.g., Floyd and Stein 2002; Rosario and Schrimshaw 2008). These are highly personal experiences that vary tremendously from person to person. Some confidently identify themselves as gay by late childhood, whereas others continue questioning and doubting their sexual identity into their 20s. For many, coming out is a smooth and natural step, but for many others, disclosing their sexual orientation is a risky and difficult enterprise. These variations notwithstanding, a common theme running through the childhood memories of many LGB individuals is the feeling of not fitting in or being somehow fundamentally different from everyone else around them (Savin-Williams and Cohen 2015, 360). This sensation takes on a more concrete form with the first experience of same-sex attraction in early or late childhood, well before puberty, setting in motion the journey toward the discovery of one's sexual orientation (Floyd and Stein 2002, 178).

The target of these first same-sex romantic and sexual ideations can be either someone in one's close environment (e.g., a schoolteacher) or a media figure (Herdt and Boxer 1993, 182–183). For example, the journalist Shane Harris describes his experiences at the age of 5 (Alter and Singleton 2017, 38):

> Though I hadn't yet conceived of my sexual identity, much less the general concept, I clearly had an instinctive fondness for boys. And Luke [Skywalker] was my favorite boy. [. . .] I couldn't look away. I loved his hair. I wondered what he looked like with his shirt off. I wanted to go on adventures with him.

Many LGB individuals recall crushes and intense emotional reactions to celebrities, particularly PSRs with Ellen DeGeneres, that guided them toward the realization of their sexual orientation (Gomillion and Giuliano 2011, 336–337). Fictional media figures can have a similar effect. For example, Howart (2019) studied lesbian fandom groups of the television science fiction action adventure series *X-Files*. Some of the women she interviewed reported that the female protagonist, Dana Scully, was their first same-sex crush, which marked their "sexual awakening" or even an experience that "made [them] lesbian" (23). Similarly, McClintock and Herdt (1996, 178) relate the story of a now 18-year-old gay man whose first realization of his sexual orientation occurred at the age of 10, he found himself sexually attracted to Captain Kirk on the television series *Star Trek*.

In my own research, in response to an open-ended question in a national survey of adults, one 18-year-old participant divulged that her most important PSRR was with Jennifer Lawrence, star of the *Hunger Games* movies. This experience at the age of 12 helped her realize that she was bisexual. Similarly, Alex (interview #20) recalled that around the same age, she too discovered that she had similar romantic feelings toward both male and female media figures. Exploring her emotions through PSRRs, she gradually came to the realization that she was bisexual.

While some LGB individuals regard their PSRRs as a pivotal component in their sexual identity development in young adolescence, for others, having a PSRR may not have been a defining moment, but merely a reaffirmation of their concealed identity. For example, in a national survey I conducted, a 42-year-old male respondent listed Ryan Phillippe in his role as Billy Douglas in the *One Life to Live* soap opera as his most important PSRR, which occurred at the age of 15. The participant indicated that he was attracted to the media figure not only because of his physique ("super hot") but also because this was the first openly gay teen character in a soap at a time he himself had not yet come out as gay.

By the time Damian (interview #17) had his first same-sex PSRR at the age of 14, he already knew he was not heterosexual. He had started questioning his sexual orientation several years prior, when he realized that he found men sexually attractive. However, growing up in a conservative family, living in a tight-knit, traditional community, and having no contact with LGB individuals, he was not sure exactly how to define himself given that he was also attracted to women. He had also experienced PSRRs with female media figures. Thus, for him, PSRRs did not facilitate the discovery of his sexual identity, but rather reaffirmed it. Because of the strong antigay sentiments in his social surroundings, Damian tried not to nurture his same-sex attraction. For example, he specifically avoided searching for information about his same-sex parasocial love interest. Nonetheless, same-sex PSRRs offered him an escape from his desolate social reality, loneliness, experience of feeling misunderstood, and emotional distress, and provided him a fanciful sexual experience as a substitution for the sexual experimentation that he could not experience in real life.

PSRRs Consistent or Inconsistent with Sexual Orientation

There is not a complete overlap between people's identification as LGB or straight and the sex of the targets of their crushes. Studies estimate that between 20% and 60% of people have had at least one crush that is inconsistent with their declared sexual orientation. In other words, many straight individuals have had a same-sex crush, and most gay and lesbian people have experienced at least one heterosexual crush (Glover, Galliher, and Lamere 2009, 88; Igartua et al. 2009, 604).

For LGB youth, some of these opposite-sex crushes could be the result of a paucity of opportunities for same-sex relationships. As discussed in chapter 5, early romantic experimentation contributes to adolescents' construction and practice of romantic scripts, thereby allowing them to develop skills that will carry over to future relationships. Growing up in an environment that is (at least perceived as) not supportive of LGBs leaves these children isolated and with fewer opportunities for romantic experiences in their immediate social circle (Glover, Galliher, and Lamere 2009). However, instead of withdrawing from the dating scene altogether (which presumably would leave them less equipped to form successful relationships later in adulthood), LGB adolescents may consider alternatives to same-sex romance: (1) the formation of same-sex, nonsexual, but particularly intimate friendships; and (2) engagement in heterosexual dating despite its incongruence with their authentic sexual orientation. These two alternatives to withdrawal were in fact found to be beneficial for LGB teens' ability to developing their relational skillset (Glover Galliher and Lamere 2009, 81–84).

Additionally, crushes inconsistent with sexual orientation can be part of a larger process of identity formation and sexual self-exploration that is fundamental to the development of both LGB and heterosexual youth. Savin-Williams and Cohen (2015, 360) note that sexual-orientation-consistent romantic and sexual attractions typically take place first, in late childhood, before puberty. Conversely, crushes that are inconsistent with the sexual orientation tend to occur later in adolescence. These later orientation-inconsistent crushes can be interpreted as a form of experimentation and a process of solidifying one's sexual self-identity. Supposedly, such crushes are meaningful for heterosexual identity development as well. While children who later identify as straight do not question their heterosexuality the way children who later identify as LGB do, they do contemplate (and reject) an LGB identity later in adolescence. Same-sex crushes at this age could be part of this phase.

To see whether the same pattern applies to PSRRs, in the survey of US adults, I asked participants if they had *ever* had a PSRR with a same-sex or an opposite-sex media figure. A large segment of the respondents (38.1%) reported having had at least one same-sex PSRR in their life. Echoing research on crushes in the nonmediated context, same-sex PSRRs do not entirely correspond to people's sexual orientation, at least the way participants defined themselves during the time of the survey. Participants were asked to identify their sexual orientation on a scale from 1 (entirely heterosexual) to 7 (entirely homosexual). Unsurprisingly, same-sex PSRRs were more common the less exclusively heterosexual they were. However, even among the 228 "entirely heterosexual" individuals in the sample, only some 80% had PSRRs solely with opposite-sex characters, while the rest of them had PSRRs with both same- and opposite-sex media figures. For 6.4% a same-sex PSRR was a one-off occurrence, but 12.4% of the "entirely heterosexual" respondents reported having had a PSRR with a same-sex character more than once. At the same time, engaging in a PSRR with an opposite-sex media figure was highly prevalent across the sexual orientation spectrum. Even of the fourteen participants who self-identified as "entirely gay," only half reported having had PSRRs exclusively with same-sex media figures.

A similar pattern of results emerged in a reanalysis of data that I collected with Sam Dorros (Tukachinsky and Dorros 2017; 2018). The analyses considered the characteristics of the most meaningful PSRRs participants had experienced in their childhood or adolescence (rather than whether they had ever had a same-sex or opposite-sex relationship over the course of their life). In the sample of teenagers, only five individuals (4.5%) had had their most important PSRR with a same-sex character. Interestingly, when asked to express their sexual orientation on a scale from 1 (entirely heterosexual) to 5 (entirely homosexual), three of these teens said they were entirely heterosexual, and one identified as equally interested in both sexes (the fifth teen skipped this question altogether). In fact, the three adolescents who viewed themselves as completely homosexual all reported that their most meaningful PSRR had been with an opposite-sex media figure.

We conducted a similar survey with college students, asking them to reflect on their PSRRs growing up. Looking back at their teenage years, nine of the 166 students who had had a PSRR experience said they had a PSRR with a same-sex media figure (5.4%). This percentage of same-sex PSRRs is close to that reported in the teenage sample. Interestingly, four of the nine students with a same-sex PSRR experience were completely or mostly homosexual, one was equally attracted to both sexes, and the other four were entirely heterosexual. Of the ten respondents who stated they are "completely homosexual," the majority (seven respondents) had a PSRR with an opposite-sex character.

Due to a small sample size, the numbers of participants in each group are rather small. However, a similar pattern emerges across both samples. Clearly, sexual orientation does not correspond perfectly with the propensity to engage in same-sex PSRRs. Gay and lesbian respondents were, in fact, less likely to have engaged in a same-sex PSRR, while self-proclaimed "entirely heterosexual" respondents did have meaningful same-sex PSRRs.

Together, these statistics demonstrate that, although heterosexual media users were less likely than LGB individuals to have same-sex PSRRs, a large share of these "exclusively straight" people had nonetheless engaged in such relationships. Similarly, the majority of LGB participants (including many who viewed themselves as entirely gay or lesbian) had had some opposite-sex PSRRs. These findings point to the possibility that PSRRs serve as an opportunity for fanciful sexual experimentation, allowing individuals to experience alternative selves and try on various sexual scripts. This survey does not offer information about the timing of these same-sex and opposite-sex relationships, but it is possible that PSRRs that do not follow one's expressed sexual orientation predate and even contribute to the solidification of one's view of oneself as heterosexual or LGB.

THE PSRR TARGET'S SEXUAL ORIENTATION

Another interesting point arises regarding LGB and heterosexual cisgender individuals' preference for LGB/heterosexual media figures. Not surprisingly, Bond (2018, 471) found that LGB adolescents were more likely to name an LGB character as their favorite media figure than heterosexual media users were. This preference was hypothesized to be driven by a need for role models, inspirational figures, and peers to assist LGB adolescents with identity development. However, that study looked at PSRs in general rather than specifically at PSRRs, which rely on other psychological mechanisms (e.g., sexual attraction) and address a different set of needs.

In my studies, it appears that LGB individuals are as likely to develop romantic PSRs with gay as with straight media figures. The interviews, however, reveal that, unique to romantic (rather than general) PSRs, the guiding principle behind the preference for a gay media figure is the ability to imagine oneself in a relationship with that personality. This was the case for both LGB and heterosexual interviewees.

When I asked the LGB interviewees about whether the media figure's sexual orientation mattered, some said they could form PSRRs with media personalities regardless because sexual orientation did not interfere with their ability to imagine becoming romantically involved with those media figures. Alex (interview #20) had no expectation or hope whatsoever for her PSRR to transpire; therefore, the sexual orientation of her parasocial love interest did not subtract from her parasocial experience. Conversely, although Damian (interview #17) had crushes on heterosexual media figures of the same sex, he preferred to invest more in his PSRRs with gay media personalities. Even though these relationships were fanciful, he also engaged in some suspension of disbelief that he could no longer sustain when the media figures were heterosexual. If the media figure were heterosexual, there would be no hope for reciprocity and his fantasy would collapse. For example, early in the interview, Damian made the rational case for why his PSRR with openly gay television personality Anderson Cooper is entirely imaginary:

> I know that I cannot meet him and I cannot have any kind of real relationship with him, and he cannot be a part of my world and I mean I cannot become a part of his world. Also because the age difference it feels to me like not something that could happen; geographically speaking it cannot happen.

But then, reflecting on why it matters to him whether his celebrity crush is straight or gay, he admits:

I would be sad to discover that they are heterosexual because there is a zero
percent chance [of a relationship with them in reality]. Like there's always a
chance of success [if he] is not hetero.

Similarly, for some heterosexual participants the sexual orientation of
their PSRR partner was consequential because eliminating any possibility
of an actual relationship demolished her ability to imagine themselves with
that media figure. For instance, Mimi (interview #22) reported that once she
learned that the social media personality she had a crush on was gay, she no
longer was able to fantasize about him because "on the whole, I wanted it to
be realistic." Becoming aware of his sexual orientation precluded any possibility of her fantasy to "realistically bump into each other in the street" and
fall in love with each other to materialize. Similarly, Allyssa's (interview
#10) crush on the actor Timothée Chalamet dissipated after she watched
the movie *Call Me by Your Name*, in which he played a gay character. She
explained that watching him in intimate same-sex scenes made her crush feel
incompatible with her new mental image of him as a gay man.

Conversely, Mika (interview #11) did not have trouble romantically relating to a straight actor playing a gay character on *Queer as Folk*. She stressed
that playing a gay character would not reduce her PSRR with the actor so
long as the actor was heterosexual, because her PSRR had to be compatible
with the target's sexual orientation:

> I cannot make this mental image of myself with someone who isn't interested
> in me because, you know, because of my gender. He's into guys? Fine! But if I
> can't imagine you and me together [. . .] it has somehow to fit into the way that
> I would be able to imagine myself in real, romantic and sexual relationships.

Ruth (interview #26) had a crush on the actor Alan Cumming, which
started with his role as the gender-fluid, bisexual MC in the Broadway musi-
cal *Cabaret* and followed him into his heteronormative role on the television
drama *The Good Wife*. Ruth admitted she had made a point of researching
the actor's personal life and felt relief when she learned that he was bisexual
rather than gay:

> The important thing is that he has a thing for women. He could be in a relation-
> ship with me. I know it is funny, silly, he is not going to be in a relationship
> with me—I know that. But somehow I cannot imagine so much being with a gay
> man. He has to be open to, be able to be interested in me as a woman for me to
> imagine being with him. Once I know he is bi, I am like, OK, great, I can really
> enjoy now fantasizing about him. [. . .] Because I know I can imagine being with
> him [. . .] I know it is possible. Even if I know it is not. He is in a relationship,
> and he doesn't know me, and I am, have my own life.

What these women articulated is that although they were fully aware of the purely imaginary nature of PSRRs, at least for some of them, their PSRRs had to have potential for reciprocity in reality in order to be enjoyable in the fantasy realm. The sexual orientation of the media figure provided the plausibility needed for the PSRR to transpire. This is particularly interesting as it presents a different experience from that of women creators and consumers of homoerotic fanfiction, known as M/M slash.

M/M Slash

M/M slash is a genre of fanfiction in which media users develop a plot depicting a romantic and sexual connection between two male characters who are not sexually or romantically involved in the original media text. One iconic example of such M/M slash is fanfiction involving Captain Kirk and Spock from *Star Trek*. Although it would be logical to assume that these narratives are developed by gay men to facilitate their same-sex PSRRs and fantasies, past research has shown that this is categorically *not* the case. While lesbian and bisexual women make up the majority of writers of femslash (fanfiction depicting a same-sex romance between two female characters) (Levin Russo 2013, 457), M/M slash is predominantly created and consumed by self-identified heterosexual women (Foster 2015, 510). Multiple studies have examined the motivation behind this practice as well as trying to understand how women derive enjoyment from such fanfiction.

M/M slash has been argued to constitute a subgenre of the romantic novel (Salmon and Symons 2004, 98). While writing targeting an audience of gay men is sexually explicit and direct, M/M slash generated by heterosexual women is more relationship oriented—described as the difference between "fucking" and "making love." It has been postulated that women choose to live their fantasies through two male characters because romantic novels inherently embody an unequal power dynamic that oppresses women. Thus, to be able to experience romance from an egalitarian point of view by identifying with either partner in the fictional romance, women may imagine themselves as one of the partners in an M/M relationship (Salmon and Symons 2004, 98). Although this is a same-sex narrative, it allows women to imagine themselves in a heterosexual relationship with either male character. Specifically, Bacon-Smith (1992, 239) claims, slash fancifully reenacts a heterosexual PSRR that the media user already has with these characters. Conversely, others have argued that M/M slash is a way for women to explore their sexual and gender identity. Through slash, women connect to their gender-fluid, gender-queer, and bisexual selves (Foster 2015, 525).

NEXT STEPS IN LGB PSRR RESEARCH

PSRR research is still in its emerging stages, and so is research on the role of PSRs in general in the sexual socialization of adolescents. Thus, much more research is needed at the intersection between these two bodies of work. Further research is needed to better understand the unique role of PSRRs (as opposed to general PSRs) in preparation for future relationships and as a substitution for lack of romantic opportunities specifically for LGB youth. Additionally, further research needs to explore the role that same-sex PSRRs play in the sexual identity development and self-realization of children and adolescents.

Chapter 8

Beyond Adolescence

PSRRs across the Life Span

Most of the research on parasocial romantic relationships (PSRRs) has focused on teenagers and young adults. However, as discussed in chapter 3, we know that PSRRs are not limited to this age group. Many individuals report experiencing PSRRs throughout their lives. PSRRs later in life may not be as potent and all-consuming as PSRRs experienced in adolescence. Nonetheless, given the tremendous variability in the intensity of PSRRs at any age, there are certainly some instances of meaningful PSRRs among emerging adults, young adults, middle-aged people, and older adults as well. How do PSRRs differ across the life span? What do they mean and what functions do they serve? To begin answering these questions, we need to first consider the psychology of life span development and understand the different roles that media-based relationships can play through the course of a person's life.

PSRS AND THEORIES OF HUMAN DEVELOPMENT

PSRs across the Life Stages

Classic psychological theories of human development (Erikson 1959; Erikson 1968; Levinson 1986) maintain that human life can be divided into several stages. Each stage has distinctive biological, psychological, and sociological characteristics, and each life stage poses unique challenges that individuals must resolve before moving on to the next stage. The transition between each stage is an important turning point. By mastering the challenges presented in each phase, individuals take another step toward building a more integrated, cohesive sense of self, what psychologists call the "ego-identity."

Only through successful resolution of the challenges posed at each life stage can a person ultimately achieve a solidified ego-identity, while unresolved challenges continue to haunt the person later in life. While Erikson's theory defines eight developmental stages from infancy to advanced adulthood, the adolescence, early adulthood, and mid-adulthood stages are particularly relevant to PSRRs.

According to Erikson, the principal challenge individuals wrestle with in adolescence is developing a distinctive identity. In this stage, children transition into adulthood by working out the tension between identity and role-confusion—actively exploring possible alternative identities or accepting the roles imposed on them by society and authority figures. This tension is what makes adolescence such a turbulent time. Children strive to establish themselves as distinct from their parents by asserting their independence and exercising greater control over their lives. Their parents, who for some teens were once all-knowing, loved, revered, and turned to because they could make everything okay, are now kicked off the pedestal, and their ideals and norms are seen as phony or stupid. But without them, adolescents find themselves in uncharted territory. And so, as young individuals reject their parents and go on a quest to define themselves on their own terms, confusion and anxiety flourish. Peers replace parents as their mental compass, and this brings a fair share of angst about fitting in, gaining social recognition from peers, and not falling behind.

This is when PSRs with media figures come to fill the void left by rejected parents, providing children with role models and inspiration (Stever 2011, 2). Studies show that adolescents' attachment to celebrities is associated with feeling more independent, being less attached to parents, and having stronger attachment to peers (Giles and Maltby 2004, 817-8). Moreover, particularly intense celebrity attachment is associated with lower self-esteem in teenagers (Chia and Poo 2009, 31–2) suggesting that those who are most fragile may seek refuge in a PSR with a celebrity. Levinson (1987, 7) refers to this preadulthood stage as a span of formative years that lay the foundation for independent adulthood. This is what makes PSRs at this stage so intense, leaving a long-lasting mark and possibly even reemerging later in life, as will be discussed here.

During the following stage, young adults strive to achieve intimacy and struggle to overcome isolation. Levinson (5) suggested that during the peak years of early adulthood, in their late 20s through late 30s, individuals experience both the most stressful and potentially satisfying aspects of their life. At this stage, individuals make the most critical decisions about family, career, and finances, and they face greater demands and obligations. Stever (2011, 2) points out the potential role of PSRRs in addressing intimacy needs and coping with loneliness. Fandom provides individuals with a meaningful social network of similar-minded individuals, offering a sense of belongingness and connection. Moreover, she argues that a PSR itself can constitute a surrogate relationship in the absence of a real one. As discussed in previous chapters, PSRs are not a substitution for relationships overall. However, given the potential of media to serve as a social surrogate to cope with an acute social threat (Derrick et al. 2009, 357–358) the substitution model may hold true specifically for particular individuals who use PSRRs to resolve this life-stage crisis.

Next, in mid-adulthood, people experience a tension between self-absorption and generativity. This stage calls for greater self-reflection and compassion, connecting to others beyond oneself. Stever (2011, 3) found that fans in this age group are more likely to be drawn to their admired celebrity's charity work. In this way, fandom becomes less self-centered and has a component of giving to the next generation, which is one of the developmental characteristics of this age group.

PSRs at Life's Turning Points

PSRs can also serve important, overarching functions that are not specific to particular life stages. Life constantly confronts individuals with new stressors; it is destabilizing. In this context, Harrington and Bielby (2010, 443–4) postulate that fandom serves an anchor—something constant to hold on to and use as a reference point. Stever (2011, 6) adds that PSRs are particularly critical during transitional points in life, not necessarily the milestones Erikson and Levinson discuss as graduating from adolescence to adulthood, but major life events that disrupt life as one knows it. Two particular turning points are considered here as a context for PSRRs: maternity and loss of a significant other.

Maternity

The birth of a child also (psychologically) signifies the birth of the baby's parents as such, transforming them and their lives forever. Daniel Stern's theory of the "motherhood constellation" articulates the psychological journey toward becoming a parent that begins during pregnancy and continues into the baby's first year of life (Stern 1995; Stern and Bruschweiler-Stern 1998). As happy and welcomed as this life event is, the milestone of parenthood is also incredibly stressful and creates an identity crisis (Barnes 2014). Becoming a mother (Stern's theory focuses on women, but it is applicable to parents of any gender) means taking on a new role that entails numerous new responsibilities and demands. They disrupt the person's existing identity components and challenge whatever notions about the self and parenthood the new parent may have had. The prospective or new mother struggles with endless fears and doubts. While most of them concern her ability to take care of and bond with the baby, the mother also has to reconsider her own identity: Who is she and what does being a mother mean for her as a woman and as a person? Reorganizing self-identity to incorporate motherhood means changing her lifestyle, making adjustments to her work routine, and altering her relationships with other important people in her life. Combined with the increased social isolation that many new mothers experience, the new role as a mother can dominate a woman's reconfigured identity and monopolize her life experience (Perun 2013, 97).

The erasure of once important identity components might be a painful loss that media can be used to ameliorate. For example, research has shown that reading romantic novels gives women license to take a pause in their lives as housewives and caretakers and dwell in a fantasy world (Radway 2009). However, PSRRs are more than self-care. They are about personal growth. In the fictional universe of a romance novel, readers can vicariously experience love and adventure and learn about the big world lying outside of what they feel like the narrow boundaries of their actual existence. Moreover, while academics have criticized romantic novels as trashy literature that brainwashes women into accepting an inferior role in society, the readers of these novels see female characters as strong and empowering. In fact, it is the male characters they regard as eye candy.

Research on romantic novel readers has showed how women identify with their female hero characters and experience the narrative world through them. PSRRs seem to take this experience to the next level. In a PSRR, the reader herself can become romantically engaged in a fantasy romance with a male character, not vicariously through a surrogate (i.e., identification with the female hero), but directly—by enacting the romance between herself and the character in her own imagination.

Several research findings speak to the role of PSRRs in reclaiming young mothers' sense of self. For example, Aubrey, Click, and Behm-Morawitz (2018) documented the phenomenon of "Twilight moms"—new mothers who develop strong parasocial (presumably romantic) relationships with the vampire character Edward in the young adult fantasy book and movie series *Twilight*. Dorsey-Elson (2016, 75) postulated that *Twilight* particularly appeals to middle-aged women because the romance reconnects them with their younger, romantic selves. It allows women to relive aspects of their girlhood, such as talking to similar-minded girlfriends about the handsome male character, and generally to escape their regular lives that are centered around caring for others.

This notion is demonstrated by the experiences recounted by Mika (interview #11), one of the women I interviewed for this book. She told me that she was watching the *Twilight* saga while nursing and breast pumping at night. Then, Mika discussed the films with other nursing women in her social milieu. All of a sudden, the career-oriented women in their 30s became teenagers again, giggling and arguing about which male character was cuter. Like Radway's romantic novel readers, Mika and her friends used *Twilight* and their crush on Edward as a fantasy space to counterbalance the demands of motherhood:

> [My friend, who also just had a baby, and I] were talking about how much time has been wasted watching the same episode again and again and talking about it and [. . .] about the characters, about the show. Like, reading other people's reviews about the show. About the same episodes that we watched like 10 times. And do that instead of laundry or actually working. And I remember saying to her then that—but that's okay because you really need it. Like, you really need that time, and that time out of life and time out of thinking about serious stuff. And I really need that, and I have to do that and I have to pretend I'm someone else and I have to go to sleep [. . .] thinking that I, um, when I wake up there's this handsome vampire that would take me in his private jet, anywhere I would want. And I have to go and think about that and not think about the baby scream- ing in the other room and all the laundry that I have.

But on a deeper level, the romantic attachment to Edward's character allowed her to diversify her self-concept, offering conversation topics and bonding with other women on a basis other than motherhood. Even more importantly, the PSRR allowed her to reclaim the sexual, younger, single, and nonmotherly self that she felt she had lost:

> We were married and we did have children at the time, there wasn't anything very sexual about that. Being reminded of the other sexuality—women's sexual- ity [. . .] that we knew there was when we were 16. [. . .] I was 32, overweight, sitting on my sofa with a baby, and another baby crying in the other room and you can't feel very sexual in that way. I do remember feeling 16.

On a deeper level, the romantic attachment to Edward's character allowed her to reclaim the sexual, younger, single, and nonmotherly self that she felt she had lost.

Loss of a Significant Other

In her interviews of fans, Stever (2011, 3) found that PSRRs often occur in adults after the loss of a significant other following a divorce or death. Losing a spouse is a debilitating experience that can leave individuals lonely and emotionally broken to the point of falling physically ill down the road (Kawai and Sasaki 2004). There is a lot to process in the death of a loved one. The Freudian approach is that healthy coping is about coming to terms with the loss and moving on, making sense of the loss and mentally reorganizing the world without the spouse. Others suggest the opposite: The goal should be not to let go of the partner but to reengage with one's memory of the deceased as part of renegotiating a new reality (Marwit and Klass 1995). Ultimately, even though the surviving spouse will forever harbor a special place in their heart for their deceased partner, life must go on. An important aspect of resuming life after losing a significant other is opening up again to the possibility of a new romantic relationship. Thus, remarriage is a healthy, adaptive behavior. However, going back into the dating scene after the loss of a significant other is hard, especially for women (Schneider et al. 1996). For example, Schneider et al. (1996) tracked widows and widowers for two years and found that while members of both groups gradually became more interested in romance and remarriage, women continued to respond to this idea with a mixture of fear and guilt. While men's fear of being romantic and their guilt about dating steadily declined over the course of two years, on average, women's levels of anxiety and guilt actually increased over this period of time (54). The percentage of bereaved women who expressed dating-related anxiety grew from 40% two months after the death of their spouse to 51% two years later, while the rate of relational anxiety among bereaved men decreased from 38% to 29% over the same time span. Similarly, on average, women's guilt subsided only slightly over the course of two years from the loss of their spouse, dwindling from 29% to 21%, while their male counterparts experienced a steep decline from 37% to 11%.

Levinson (1997) charted the long and multi-phased journey toward readjustment for young widows. First, Levinson claimed, mourning is all-consuming, as women experience loneliness and devastation in full. When the mourning becomes less central to the widow's existence, she starts reentering the world, reengaging in new activities, and enjoying small pleasures. However, reentering the dating scene is still awkward and emotionally painful, rendering the first relationship very fragile and transient, yet extremely important. In Levinson's words (283):

> The first intimate encounter is paramount for the young widow because it revalidates her sensuality and sexuality as a woman. It gives her a dimension she has not experienced since before her husband's death. It demonstrates a sense of self, separate and apart from her marital relationship. It thrusts her into the world of the living from the world of the dead. She allows herself to lower the walls blocking her emotions so that she can again experience feelings.

These first relationships tend to dissolve after a short period of time, and the partner in these relationships is not significant, Levinson argues, but the relationship itself is crucial for the adjustment process and constitutes a milestone signifying the woman's reorganization of her sense of self. Thus, this first relationship prepares the woman for the more enduring, healthy relationships to come in the next stage of the adjustment journey.

Conceivably, for some women, PSRRs serve the role of this first post-loss romance. They can be particularly important for women who are in greater need of easing the readjustment process. PSRRs may allow them to safely rediscover their romantic self and gradually become more comfortable with being attached to someone other than the deceased spouse.

Allegra's (interview #24) experience provides support for this assertion from another angle. Allegra had multiple intense PSRRs throughout her life, beginning in her early teens and extending well into her 30s. However, in her early 40s, after her 19-year-long marriage came to an end in a bitter divorce, her PSRRs ceased too:

> I do not want a man in my life. Absolutely not. Don't even go there. It may be that has affected me not forming a crush on a male actor because I am so adamant that I do not want to deal with a man right now.

Her account suggests that PSRRs can constitute a component in a readjustment process preparing the media user for reengaging in real-world romantic relationships. Allegra appeared to still be relatively early in this process, and thus may not have been ready for even a parasocial romantic experience. However, arguably, over time, Allegra would reconnect with her romantic self and start developing romantic feelings toward media figures, which would pave the road to her reentry to the dating scene in real life.

It is not about media figures offering company through a surrogate relationship. Rather, these relationships help individuals to piece together their shattered sense of self. After losing their significant other, they feel that their ability to love and engage in romance is lost too. But having a PSRR allows them to be in touch with their feelings again. "I didn't think I could feel this way about anyone again," several interviewees told Stever (2011, 3), reflecting on their PSRRs following the loss of their significant others. They were coming to the realization that while their spouses were dead, they were not, and that they were free to reengage with life.

EVOLUTION OF THE NOTION OF "SELF"

The previous sections outlined two theoretical approaches to PSRs across the life span that articulate the role of PSRs in different life stages and during formative life events. Both approaches highlight the role of PSRs in identity formation and maintenance. People integrate their media experiences into their self-narratives, and these experiences become part of the story of who they are, where they come from, and where they are going.

Interestingly, this process can work in two opposite ways—someone may revisit and embrace past PSRs or may reject them and become an anti-fan. As part of anti-fandom, individuals reflect on their past PSRs and "sober up," becoming disenchanted. Some have a condescending (even if forgiving) view of their younger self who was "obsessed" with a celebrity. This contrast with one's younger self is a reminder of how much one has matured, grown, evolved, and become more sophisticated. For example, older individuals whom I have interviewed (e.g., 73-year-old Rochelle, interview #18) attributed their difficulty developing PSRs and becoming absorbed in fictional stories by stating that as they grew older they became harder to entertain and less naïve.

Conversely, Stever (2010) found that some individuals rediscover their youth fandom and that rekindling their PSR allows them to reconnect to their younger self. In other words, instead of drawing a contrast between their young, foolish, obsessed self and their current mature, sophisticated self, these fans can feel young again by reliving some aspects of their youth. Harrington and Bielby (2020, 440, 444) found that individuals who hold on to their fandom feel that this additional dimension to their routine family and work is what gives their life meaning.

For others, a PSRR is a way to revisit and reconnect with a lost aspect of their past. For example, Sierra's (interview #12) first encountered Josh Groban when she was in her 50s, around the time when her husband of more than three decades moved into a nursing home. Her husband had been diagnosed with Alzheimer's disease for almost a decade at that point, and the illness had slowly robbed Sierra of the man she loved until he no longer recognized her. She longed for him and found a connection in listening to Groban's romantic songs and talking back to him:

> It's somewhat like how I used to talk with my husband. I'd share stuff with him, you know. Then, I used to be able to have that relationship. But now that I don't [. . .] and I do that with Josh's music.

She found consolation in this PSR, which allowed her to reconnect to her younger self: "It brings back times, you know, happy, happy times in my life, not so much like it is now."

PSRR also serves as a strategy for coping with a midlife crisis that involves reevaluation of the choices the media users have made in their life that had brought them to where they were now and reconsidering the alternative paths not taken. Connecting to one's teenage self is a reminder of the dreams and opportunities one considered when all doors were still open. Women interviewees reported that the PSRRs repositioned their ego in a central role after it had been shoveled to the curbside while they were focusing on raising a family and running a household.

For example, for Cathy (interview #19), who was 54 years old at the time I interviewed her, rekindling her teenage PSRR at the age of 48 was part of a bigger identity crisis. She had been an "extreme mom," devoted to her family. But when her children grew up and her marital relationship started deteriorating, she felt that "I had to find who I was. I had to really, like, start discovering again who [Cathy] is. Not the mother, not the girlfriend." It was then that Cathy reconnected to her teenage PSRR, Bruce Dickson: "He has been the constant in my life. No matter who I was. Well, guess what? I can always go back to Bruce." Rekindling a PSRR with the heavy metal star—her high school parasocial sweetheart—and following him on a tour allowed her to claim her individual self.

Rochelle's (interview #18) only PSRR took place shortly after separating from her husband following a long, toxic relationship. She described this experience as something highly atypical of herself. "Everyone who knew me was surprised," she recounted. She was known to be a down-to-earth, no-nonsense person. Having a crush on someone who was not a viable romantic candidate seemed to go against her notion of herself and the self-image she had projected to others. However, in the new bleak reality of her life, as a single mother to a young child, facing financial insecurity, her infatuation with the actor not only diverted her attention, at least partially, from these stressors but also energized her and infused her life (and self-concept) with another layer of meaning.

Falling in love with a character has a rejuvenating effect; it makes a media user feel like a 17-year-old again. Cathy's PSRR allowed her to feel intense emotions that she had in her teen years. Ultimately, PSRRs are a self-transcending experience. As Dorsey-Elson, a scholar and a self-proclaimed "Twilight mom" concluded in her autoethnography,

"[I] know my place in a universe in a way that finally works. I am more whole now than I have been in my adult years, and I have a fictional 17-year-old teen-age girl, a 107-year-old vampire and a young-adult fiction author, Stephenie Meyer, to thank for it" (2016, 76).

We know from research on social relationships that romantic engagements can have a profound effect on our personal growth. People expand their mental representation of who they are, their own identity and self-perception, to include their significant other (Aron, Paris, and Aron 1995). In other words, we tend to think of ourselves as encompassing some of our partners' characteristics. And since we tend to be attracted to people who embody qualities we wish to possess ourselves, this psychological merging with our partners also brings us closer to our ideal selves.

Moreover, both consciously and not, people in a relationship create opportunities for their partners to act on their ideals or inhibit behaviors they wish to extinguish. They then offer their partners feedback (again, not always in full awareness) that encourages the partners to keep up the good work and continue working toward those ideals. Simply put, an individual in a relationship is motivated and enabled to take action to become the person they wish to be. This cycle of self-improvement, dubbed "the Michelangelo Phenomenon" has been extensively documented in research (Drigotas 2002; Drigotas et al. 1999). Although theoretically the gap between one's ideal and actual selves is driven by a feedback loop, through an interaction between both partners, it is also possible for this process to apply to PSRs as well, even though they lack two-way interactions. For example, research on PSRs in general has found that being reminded of one's favorite celebrity makes individuals with low self-esteem feel closer to the ideal self they want to be (Derrick, Gabriel, and Tippin 2008). This suggests that even without being directly affirmed by their media-based significant others, individuals can feel more self-fulfilled just by thinking of their PSRR-target.

CONCLUDING THOUGHTS

PSRRs seem to play a major role at critical points in people's lives, such as when they are standing at major life intersections or unhinged by a major life crisis. As media users reflect on how to navigate through such turmoil, PSRRs offer them a reminder of who they are, what they strive to be, what is important to them, and that they possess the strength they need to overcome these challenges. PSRRs are also some of the building blocks of identity and connection to others. Ruth (interview #26) described her experience of falling in love with an actor when she was a married mother in her late 30s as "a secret part of me not known to anyone else in my life." She cherished this special dimension of her life that was just hers to savor. Fifty-four-year-old Cathy (interview #19), on the other hand, shared that she loved displaying her crush on Bruce Dickson (a heavy metal music artist) as a nonconformist, eccentric side of herself in order to shock the people around her: "People were like, why you're doing this, Chanel girl?" She felt that "it just makes me cool." She expanded her sense of self by adding another layer to her predictable, socially conforming identity:

So it [the PSRR] becomes such a part of who I am that if anything's gonna define me, like, I have no problem with that because it catches people off guard. [. . .] So it becomes part of who you are and what defines you. And if anything's gonna define me—I love that.

Chapter 9

Too Much Love Will Kill You?

PSRRs between Normalcy and Dysfunction

A boy meets a girl. A boy wants to win the girl.

The boy was 21-year-old John Hinckley—a college dropout and aspiring, broke songwriter who moved around the country failing to kick-start his career. The girl was Jodie Foster, a teen actress who already had a few movies on her resume when she made her major breakthrough in the 1976 *Taxi Driver*. In that film, Foster played a 12-year-old sex worker cared for by Robert De Niro's character, a troubled man who was contemplating a political assassination.

The boy met the girl in the movie. Hinckley was obsessed with *Taxi Driver*. He watched it fifteen times in the theater and was infatuated with Foster. Hinckley showered the young actress with numerous letters and poems professing his love and called her a few times on the phone. But Foster did not reciprocate.

To win the girl, Hinckley decided he would assassinate the President of the United States. He swindled money from his parents, claiming he needed money to enroll in a composition class at Yale University. He then used the funds to fly around the country following President Jimmy Carter and to go to New Haven seeking contact with Foster, who had just started her freshman year at Yale. Hinckley was not successful at approaching President Carter, but he had more luck with his successor.

Three months into his presidency, on March 30, 1981, President Ronald Reagan was scheduled to address a labor union at the Washington Hilton Hotel. His schedule was publicized in the *Washington Star*, and Hinckley traveled to the hotel a few days prior to the event. In his last letter to Foster, Hinckley confided in her:

Jodie, I would abandon this idea of getting Reagan in a second if I could only win your heart and live out the rest of my life with you, whether it be in total obscurity or whatever. I will admit to you that the reason I'm going ahead with this attempt now is because I just cannot wait any longer to impress you. I've got to do something now to make you understand in no uncertain terms that I am doing all of this for your sake. By sacrificing my freedom and possibly my life I hope to change your mind about me. This letter is being written an hour before I leave for the Hilton Hotel. Jodie, I'm asking you to please look into your heart and at least give me the chance with this historical deed to gain your respect and love.

That fateful Monday afternoon, the president was on schedule. After the speech, he was hastened to his limousine down the President's Walk—a passage intentionally designed as a secure point of exit from the hotel. The president dismissed the directive to wear a bulletproof vest, however. After all, this was a mere 30-foot walk in a venue specifically chosen for its superbly secure design, which was built after the 1963 assassination of President John F. Kennedy. Unsuspectingly, President Reagan passed by Hinckley. He waived to the applauding crowd and stood by the car taking questions from the press. It was then that Hinckley fired his pistol, discharging all six rounds of ammunition in less than two seconds. The first bullets wounded the press secretary, a police officer, and a Secret Service agent who jumped to take the bullet. The other bullets also missed a direct hit at the president but the last one ricocheted from the limousine and struck the president's left lung missing his heart by just a few inches.

Finally, the president was rushed to the hospital, where he underwent a life-saving surgery. Upon his survival of the assassination attempt, his approval rating surged to 73 percent. Hinckley was apprehended and put on trial. He insisted that Foster testify in court. Ultimately, she complied and testified in a closed session, to Hinckley's delight. He has been quoted exclaiming: "Mom! Dad! I'll be right there in the *same room!*" During the court proceedings, Foster was asked to describe her relationship with Hinckley. "I don't have any relationship with John Hinckley," she replied flatly. After three days of deliberations, the jury delivered a verdict of "not guilty by reason of insanity." Hinckley spent the following decades at St. Elizabeth's Hospital in Washington D.C. until his release in 2016. Foster, who went on to become one of the most acclaimed actors and directors in Hollywood, rarely spoke about her stalker again, refusing to take questions about the incident in interviews.

Hinckley's story is the epitome of pathological fandom and parasocial romantic relationships (PSRRs). PSRRs, as part of a broader concept of fandom, have been historically viewed as delusional experiences that pose a threat to both the person's own psychological well-being and the society at large. In their mild form, PSRRs are believed to displace real-life relationships, breeding noncompliance with societal romantic and sexual norms. In extreme cases, PSRRs are presumed to be dangerous, even murderous, as is exemplified by Hinckley's story. Such derogatory views of fandom have dominated the scholarship in this field for decades and are still prevalent in the social and cultural discourse, driving the public's attention to marginal, extreme, and unrepresentative examples of these phenomena. They cultivate stigmas of fans as social misfits who are asexual, sexually deviant, mentally ill, or dangerous. Since these stigmas misrepresent the place of PSRRs in the lives of most people who experience them, it is important to understand the concerns raised about PSRRs and examine these claims empirically. What makes a PSRR pathological? At what point does a romantic PSR cross the line from normal to dysfunctional? What pushes PSRRs over the edge? And how common are pathological PSRRs?

THE PATHOLOGICAL PERSPECTIVE

Fandom as a Pathology

The word "fandom" itself originates from "fanaticism," which refers to excessive religious devotion. More recently, the term has been applied to a secular context in reference to idol-like worshiping of celebrities (McDayter 2009, 149–50). The origins of the word raise connotations of obsession, delusion, and hysteria. As the argument goes, fandom is cultivated by low levels of self-worth and weak ego boundaries. Fans are loners—that is to say, they are losers because they fail to form and maintain "authentic" relationships. These socially inept individuals feel deprived of meaningful connections and seek social recognition, esteem, and autonomy. They fulfill these needs vicariously by merging with the celebrity they worship and sharing that celebrity's status and power. Much as the compensation hypothesis predicts (discussed in chapter 5), fans' fantasy relationships are viewed as substitutions for real relationships they are unsuited to have in "real" life.

Against this backdrop, as fandom became a subject of scientific research, scholars used several clinical mental health constructs to theorize celebrity worshiping (Maltby et al. 2002; Maltby et al. 2006; McCutcheon et al. 2002). First, they argue, fans display symptomology of obsessive compulsive disorder in their excessive commitment to collecting any piece of information about the target of their PSR, accumulating memorabilia, and constantly thinking about the media figure. Second, these obsessive behaviors and thoughts can also be seen as a form of addiction, no different from out-of-control gambling and online gaming. Third, fandom involves psychological disassociation. Fans lose their own identity and merge with that of the celebrity, sometimes even adopting the behaviors, clothing, or speech of the person they admire. In the case of PSRRs, the fan may assume the identity of the onscreen romantic partner of the character they have a crush on. Hinckley, for example, emulated the appearance, mannerisms, and assassination ideations of De Niro's character who starred opposite Foster in *Taxi Driver*. Finally, arguably, fandom entails detachment from reality. The relationship between a fan and their idol is entirely imaginary, and thus it is based on supposedly unhealthy levels of fantasy and absorption. Supporters of this view claim that "normative" fandom is a mild form of dangerously pathological fandom. The line between normal and pathological is fuzzy, and fans are always at risk for being pushed over the edge into the realm of pathology (Jenson 1992, 11).

PSRRs as a Pathology

Not all "pathological" expressions of fandom, including stalking and violence, have a romantic undercurrent (e.g., John Lennon's assassin was an admirer who idealized and tried to emulate Lennon, but had no romantic affinity toward him). However, PSRRs have not been spared from pathologization. To the contrary, extreme PSRRs, especially ones involving a celebrity target, can be formally diagnosed as manifestations of a mental disorder called "erotomania." The concept of erotomania, or "raving love" in Greek, dates back to ancient Greece and Rome, appearing in the writings of Hippocrates and Plutarch. It was adopted as a French medical term in 1741 and migrated to English in 1874 (Berrios and Kennedy 2002, 383). In 1987, the third revised *Diagnostic and Statistical Manual of Mental Disorders* (*DSM-III-R*), published by the American Psychiatric Association, identified erotomania as a discrete subtype of delusional disorder. It is still listed in the current version of the *DSM-V*, published in 2013; however, it is not included among other mental and behavioral disorders in the World Health Organization's manual for *International Statistical Classification of Diseases and Related Health Problems* (*ICD*).

Erotomania is defined as a romantic or sexual fixation on a love interest in a person of a higher status (e.g., a celebrity, boss, physician) to the point that it consumes the patient's life. A person with erotomania makes repeated, escalating attempts to approach his or her supposed lover and is not deterred by rejection. In fact, one of the hallmarks of erotomania is maintaining the conviction of being loved in return despite evidence to the contrary. To uphold the delusion of requited love and certitude that the relationship will transpire, a person with erotomania systematically misinterprets the target's expressions of disinterest. For example, the clinical literature describes a case study of a woman who made multiple international trips in an attempt to come in contact with a popular rock musician she was in love with (Garland and McGennis 1998, 23). Demanding to see him, she proclaimed:

> We're supposed to be having a relationship but we can only do it by telepathy at the moment. [. . .] I know he loves me—he isn't here because he wants me to sort out my head first. [. . .] [The band's] latest album was released on my birthday—that was a sign.

The distinction between excessive but not clinically pathological love and a "love disorder" lies in the intensity of this experience and its delusional aspect. Specifically, some mental health professionals maintain that "normal" love is inherently based on reciprocity. Thus in normal circumstances, unrequited love gradually dissipates, whereas morbid infatuation persists without mutual interest and occupies a central part of the person's life (Mullen and Pathe 1994, 614).

Not all individuals with erotomania engage in stalking. However, for those who do, persisting rejection can escalate erotomanic stalking from a nuisance to life-threatening violence. Such violence can be sparked by a number of factors. First, individuals with erotomania might grow jealous of others they presume to be competing with them for the supposed lover's affection. Second, individuals with erotomania can be violent toward those they believe to stand between them and their loved one, sabotaging their union. It has been suggested that projecting the love target's rejection to such third parties enables the person with erotomania to maintain the delusion of mutual love. They can continue to idealize their target and even view the act of violence as a way to protect or rescue their loved one. Finally, when the realization of rejection does sink in, the embarrassment presents an unbearable blow to the person's sense of self. This is not surprising considering that erotomania often occurs in individuals with a narcissistic personality, who are very proud and hypersensitive yet shaky in their sense of self-regard. Moreover, since their entire sense of self is fixated on their love target, rejection pulls the rug out from under their entire existence. And so, shuttering the fantasy transforms infatuated love into violent fury (Meloy 1998 614–6). Notably, erotomania has been diagnosed in both sexes and across sexual orientation categories. However, while it is estimated to be more common in women, men are overrepresented in criminal cases involving erotomania (Brüne 2003, 86).

The case of Madonna's stalker, Robert Hoskins, constitutes a famous illustration of what appears to be such a violent case of erotomania (although no information about his formal diagnosis is publicly available). Hoskins was an adult when he developed a sudden obsession with Madonna and told several people that she was his wife (Meloy 1998, 37–41; Saunders and Wainwright 2008, Ch. 2). In April 1994, he trespassed on her property twice and demanded to see her, though she was not on premises at the time. He left her bodyguard, Basil Stephens, and her personal assistant, Caresse Henry, a note written on a religious pamphlet condemning fornication outside marriage and citing it as a capital offense. The note read, "I love you. Will you be my wife for keeps." He then threatened to kill the bodyguard if he failed to deliver the message to Madonna and promised to "slice her throat from ear to ear" if she turned down his marriage proposal. Madonna returned home just three minutes after Hoskins's departure. In fact, she passed right by him on her bike, but Hoskins did not recognize her. He returned to Madonna's property seven weeks later and after a struggle with the bodyguard, regained control of a pistol and shot him.

He was apprehended in April 1995 and was charged with making terrorist threats against Madonna, Stephens, and Henry; stalking Madonna; and assaulting Stephens. While awaiting sentencing, Hoskins adorned his cell with graffiti reading "Madonna love me." When asked by the judge whether he had received any mental health treatment while imprisoned, Hoskins responded that no treatment was necessary since "there was nothing wrong with me" (Meloy 1998, 42). The judge dismissed the psychiatric evaluation and sentenced Hoskins to ten years in prison, which he served in its entirety. As he approached the end of his term, Hoskins underwent another psychological evaluation, which determined that he still posed a substantial threat to others. Thus, upon release from jail he was placed in Atascadero State Hospital, a maximum-security psychiatric facility (Saunders and Wainwright 2008, Ch. 2).

PSRR Pathology beyond Stalking

Hinckley and Hoskins embody the "crazed" male fan stereotype of a violent, potentially homicidal stalker. But even completely benign forms of PSRRs that do not entail violence or delusion of reciprocity are stigmatized as excessive, posing a threat to the person's psychological well-being and destroying relationships and families. For instance, Vermorel (2011, Ch. 1) presents letters from women fans who divulge their infatuation with the music artist Barry Manilow. One of the women, for example, describes fantasizing about Manilow during sexual intercourse with her husband. Another fan recounts that her friend's obsession with Manilow was so excessive that the friend's husband confronted her with an ultimatum: Manilow or their marriage. The woman allegedly chose a divorce.

In line with the substitution hypothesis, PSRRs are deemed to be an escape from reality into an unhealthy fantasy. They therefore perpetuate a vicious cycle wherein lonely and socially inept individuals devoid themselves from any opportunity to form real intimacy and ultimately become even more divorced from reality.

Consider, for example, the otaku subculture of Japanese animation fandom. Manga (graphic novels) and anime (animated videos and video games) originated from children's entertainment but have evolved into a complex art form encompassing various subgenres and spanning science fiction, action, and explicit sexual material. The narratives feature complex plotlines, development of well-rounded characters, and sophisticated intertextual iconography. By the 1970s and 1980s, anime and manga had become a major cultural phenomenon in Japan (Guo and Zeng 2018, 480–3). Gaining global popularity, it swiftly grew into a multimillion-dollar industry in the United States, Europe, and Southeast Asia (Bryce et al. 2010).

Despite the growing popularity of these art forms and their entrance into mainstream American culture, manga and anime fans, like members of many other fandom communities, are subjected to stigmatization and marginalization. Similarly to how *Star Trek* fans were pejoratively dubbed "Trekkies," Japanese animation fans, particularly young males, are referred to as *otaku*, which roughly translates from Japanese as "nerd" or "geek" with (at least initially[1]) a derogatory connotation. Members of this community face stereotypes such as being "losers," "weird," and "ugly" (Guo and Zeng 2018, 484) and are believed to be obsessed with fantasy animation to escape reality because they lack basic social skills (Reysen et al. 2017).

Fans often develop strong, long-lasting romantic attachment to the animated protagonists of their favorite shows. The target of one's parasocial love is referred to as a *waifu* or *hasbado*—a phonographic representation of how a native Japanese speaker would pronounce the English words "wife" and "husband," respectively. They form complex emotional and erotic relationships with these characters that are no less meaningful than relationships with individuals in the physical world (*3D* vs. *2D people*, in their jargon). For example, a Reddit community devoted to the subject enforces monogamy, not only prohibiting multiple simultaneous PSRRs but also banning having a romance with "3D people" while engaged with an anime character (r/ waifuism Rules, n.d. https://www.reddit.com/r/waifuism/).

A well-oiled merchandise industry facilitates PSRRs by offering various representations of characters, from plastic action figures, to cute plush dolls, to dakimakuras—full-body-size huggable pillows featuring a hypersexualized, at times almost pornographic depiction of the character. According to Character Databank Ltd.'s 2018 "Character Impressions Survey," some 82% of people in Japan owned some kind of character product (Gatebox, n.d.). Some fans possess multiple versions of their waifu's representation to be used for different occasions, and they spend lavishly on gifts—both virtual and physical accessories—for their beloved characters.

In 2016, the Japanese startup Vinclu launched Gatebox, a virtual assistant (akin to Amazon's Echo) that enables an otaku to engage in a more interactive and lifelike relationship with their waifu. The company's slogan, "Living with Characters: A World Where the Real and the Fictional Live Side-By-Side," captures their vision of using technology to break the boundaries that constrain fictional characters to two-dimensional realms and integrate them into the everyday lives of their admirers (https://www.gatebox.ai/en/corporate/about). The Gatebox, initially priced at close to $3,000, constitutes an 8-inch-tall cylindrical container equipped with cameras, sensors, and speakers, powered by Colva's AI technology. It projects a 3D hologram of one of the popular anime characters inside the jar or can be hooked to a TV. The device is small enough to be carried around, and so the character can offer her "master" (in waifu-speak) company throughout the day, from waking him up in the morning to being by his side at dinnertime. Furthermore, with the help of anime voice actress Yuka Saitō, the hologramic waifu is capable of carrying out basic conversations, such as asking her master about how his day went, urging him to go to bed early, and even sending him affectionate messages throughout the day.

Fostering their clients' infatuation, in 2017 Gatebox started offering marriage certificates to sanctify the interdimensional relationship between otakus and their waifus. Although it appears that the service has been discontinued, the company reportedly issued more than 3,700 certificates in its first year of offering the service (Jozuka 2018; Vice 2018). Cross-dimensional marriages are not legally recognized, yet according to some news reports, several Japanese companies encourage their employees to marry their waifu or husbado, providing them with perks such as a roughly $50 monthly marriage benefit stipend and a day off on the fictional character's birthday (Bayle 2017).

Several cross-dimensional weddings have made international headlines. First, in 2010, a 28-year-old South Korean, Lee Jin-gyu, allegedly married the magical television anime series character Fate Testarossa. The character's image was printed on a dakimakura pillow that was fitted with a wedding gown for the occasion (Daily Telegraph 2010). In a 2018 ceremony, the Tokyo-based 35-year-old school administrator Akihiko Kondo (pictured in Figure 9.1) cemented his PSRR with the Gatebox hologramic 16-year-old virtual reality and anime character Hatsune Miku. At the reception, attended by almost forty guests, Miku was represented by an 18-inch stuffy (Jozuka 2018).

Some reports make such intense PSRRs appear normative and commonplace among anime fans. In a BBC interview, the sociologist Masahiro Yamada revealed that according to his research, some 12% of his survey respondents had reported falling in love with anime characters (BBC 2018). The *New York Times* reported that the culture of 2D love is Japan linking the phenomenon to a high percent of virgins among individuals in their thirties (Katayama 2009). However, despite the media-celebrated examples of fans who blur the line between imaginary realms and reality, they probably compose only a small fraction of the overall population. Nor do these

Figure 9.1   Akihiko Kondo, Posing with His Marriage Certificate and a Doll Representing his Wife, the Virtual Reality Idol and Anime Character, Hatsune Miku. *Source:* Courtesy of BEHROUZ MEHRI/AFP via Getty Images.

individuals constitute the mainstream. A YouTube video featuring a man taking his waifu dakimakura on rides in a theme park and ordering her a full dinner at a restaurant captures reactions of other patrons and service providers ranging from disbelief and bemusement to discomfort and pity (TrueCloud9999 2010). Several comments in Korean posted in response to the video lament that the uncharacteristic portrayal is an embracement to their culture. Examination of the discussions on waifu online communities similarly reflects self-awareness on behalf of the community members. They do not confuse reality with fiction, but, for various personal reasons, make a conscious choice to favor a relationship with a fictional character over "3D." Realizing that their choices are not socially common, many prefer to limit the discussion and disclosure of their feelings to other members of the community.

CHALLENGING THE PATHOLOGICAL APPROACH

As a counterbalance to the popular cultural and academic view of fandom as a pathology, fan-centered scholarship emerged in the 1990s to make the case for legitimizing fandom. Broadly speaking, there are three arguments in defense of PSRRs: (1) Traditional scholarship overlooks the power of fans, who are not loners doped or brainwashed by media but rather a meaningful community engaged in an active and creative process; (2) scholars from a pathological fandom perspective generalize rare and nonrepresentative instances of mental conditions manifested in extreme PSRRs to cast a shadow on what is, in fact, a normative phenomenon; and (3) the discourse surrounding PSRRs is culturally insensitive, and cultural bias leads to stigmatization and marginalization of an otherwise healthy human behavior. The following sections consider each of these arguments in defense of fandom and PSRRs as a normative process.

Fans Are Not Culturally Doped

Scholars like Jenkins (1992) maintain that fans take ownership of mass-produced cultural messages and exercise their agency to inject them with their own meaning. Fans often do so through fan art, such as slash videos—creating a montage of *Star Trek* movie scenes to generate a narrative featuring a same-sex affair between protagonists that were not romantically involved in the original text. From this perspective, fandom is a far cry from a loner's mindless obsession. Rather, it is an intricate social practice connecting same-minded individuals in an effort to actively construct a meaningful, shared culture. These are not loners, "weirdos," and social misfits who fail in their personal lives and are brainwashed by media. Much to the contrary, fans constitute a vibrant and tight community where cultural creativity often defies the mass culture industry. In fact, the crusade against fandom could be attributed to the mainstream media industry, which may feel threatened by the power of these fans. The portrait of fans as active and socially integrated individuals stands in direct contrast to the violent fan image painted by the pathological model that describes fans as delusional and narcissistic (Meloy 1999, 423) suffering from an "empty self" and identity diffusion (e.g., Houran, Navik, and Zerrusen 2005; Jenson 1992, 17; Reeves, Baker, and Truluck 2012).

Fandom Behaviors Are Not "Symptoms"

Fandom researchers such as Gayle Stever, who spent several decades studying *Star Trek* and Michael Jackson's fans, believe that the attempt to pathologize fandom does grave injustice to fan communities. Stever (2011, 1357; 2020, 74) laments that committed fans would score high on measures of "symptoms" designed by fandom researchers such as Maltby and McCutcheon, who come from a fandom-as-pathology tradition (Maltby et al. 2002; Maltby et al. 2006; McCutcheon et al. 2002). However, looking only at truly pathological aspects of that scale, it is clear that behaviorally committed fans do not exhibit border-pathological behaviors any more than the general population. Rather, fans are, with rare exceptions, well-adjusted individuals who enjoy rich, healthy, and satisfying social relationships outside the PSR context. Her research demonstrates that truly pathological fan behaviors are extremely rare and generally occur among individuals with underlying mental health issues.

Even within the psychiatric medical community, the status of erotomania as a discrete disorder has been contested. Clearly, extreme infatuation or delusional conviction in being loved in return can be mere manifestations of a more general underlying mental health condition, such as schizophrenia or bipolar disorder. To be considered as a disorder in its own right, symptoms of erotomania should be present in patients with no other mental diagnosis (Brunskill 2017). This primary, pure, form of erotomania has been thought to emerge from social contexts (e.g., absence of a father figure) or a premorbid personality—in individuals who are socially inept, isolated, and incapable of sustaining intimacy, characteristics which are sometimes disguised by pride and belief in their superiority (Mullen and Pathe 1994).

In theory, it should be easy to identify whether erotomania symptoms are present in individuals who otherwise do not have any mental health conditions. However, in actuality the picture is much muddier, and it proves difficult to distinguish between erotomania as a symptom of another condition and a stand-alone diagnosis (e.g., Brunskill 2017; Garland and McGennis, 1998). Anderson et al. (1998) review the literature on neurological manifestations of erotomania and uncover that erotomania can emerge following damage to the frontal lobe as a result of conditions that cause deterioration of brain matter, such as hemorrhages, brain tumors, Alzheimer's disease, dementia, and alcoholism. Moreover, erotomanic symptoms are almost always coupled with diagnosis of other mental conditions.

Going back to the example of Hinckley, strictly speaking, he did not meet the criteria for primary erotomania because while he was infatuated with Foster, he had no delusion of being loved in return. Rather, his erotamanic symptoms were merely a manifestation of the several personality disorders he had: schizoid, narcissistic, borderline, and passive-aggressive. Even Madonna's stalker, Hoskins, who seemed to present many symptoms of erotomania, was unlikely to have had it as a primary condition. Saunders and Wainwright (2008, Ch. 2) review Hoskins's earlier life as described by his brother, Mike. The account reveals the presence of many psychopathic characteristics. Hoskins was described as someone who "has no fear," "had no fear of authority," and had "always been violent" (124); past actions included beating his sister, threatening to kill his parents, and growing up to be an abusive husband and father. In his youth, Hoskins stole cars and once attacked a police officer on duty. Moreover, he suffered from substance dependency, including use of morphine in adolescence and methamphetamine in adulthood. Thus, although Hoskins's amorous behaviors meet DSM's criteria for erotomania, it would likely be classified as a secondary expression of the other disorders rather than a stand-alone condition.

Cultural Insensitivity

Finally, the cultural and medical discourse of fandom and PSRRs can be viewed as culturally biased and failing to recognize its cultural blind spots. Even within the medical field, the definition of erotomania has sparked some controversy. While researchers and mental health practitioners agree that some extreme instances clearly represent a delusional disorder, most cases of erotomania fall within a wide gray area, making it hard to draw the line between pathological and normative infatuation (Mullen and Pathe 1994). Some have campaigned to exclude sexual disorders from the *DSM* altogether, arguing that the diagnosis criteria reflect cultural and value-laden judgments rather than being driven by scientific data (Moser and Kleinplatz 2006).

The disparaging view of PSRRs intersects with stereotypes of other underprivileged social groups. Approaching PSRRs as a clinical condition, for example, reflects gendered and traditional family values. In the medical literature, erotomania has been dubbed an "old maid's insanity" (Anderson et al. 1998, 331), and its primary variant has been argued to result, at least in part, from absence of a father figure (Mullen and Pathe 1994, 161, 620). Similarly, the American mainstream media's condescending discourse of the waifu/husbado culture propagates conformity with traditional family values and sexual norms coupled with Asian stereotypes, such as obsession with technology and sexual deviance. Research on "2D love" has to be approached without judgment, with greater cultural sensitivity, and appreciation for sexual diversity, including a spectrum of asexuality and its "fictioromantic" variant (Yule, Brotto and Gorzalka 2017).

FINAL WORDS

Taken together, then, PSRRs are not inherently problematic, nor do they represent a precarious slippery slope. Contrary to the pathological view of fandom, PSRRs do *not* have the potential to grow from "normal" fandom to a dangerous obsession. On the contrary, fandom and PSRRs are normative and commonplace. Surely, like any other human activity, they can be an outlet for manifestation of a preexisting disorder. Only a tiny subset of fans will be delusional, sincerely expecting the celebrity to reciprocate their infatuation, whereas the vast majority engage in meaningful and strong PSRRs with media figures without any negative implications for their psychological well-being. For some individuals, these relationships offer invaluable emotional and social resources. Nonetheless, the conceptual and operational definitions employed by researchers who approach fandom from a mental health perspective cast a stigma on the entire fandom community by failing to adequately discriminate between normative, playful processes and presentation of mental disorders that are not inherent to fandom but are merely exhibited in this context.

Given the pervasiveness of PSRs, other normative theoretical approaches to PSRRs have emerged, focusing on the functions that these relationships fulfill, specifically considering the motivations driving them and their consequences, both pro-social and maladaptive.

NOTE

1. The fandom community later adopted this term to refer to themselves, taking ownership of this word and neutralizing its meaning.

Chapter 10

And in the End

PSRR Dissolution

Relatively little empirical research has investigated why, how, and with what effect parasocial relationships (PSRs) come to an end. However, we do know that just as fanciful relationships with media figures are powerful psychological experiences, so is their termination, provoking disappointment, anger, missing of the media persona, and loneliness. The following sections will discuss theories and empirical data concerning parasocial breakups (PSBs) overall, then apply them specifically to the context of romantic PSBs.

PARASOCIAL BREAKUPS: WHY DO PSRS END?

To start, it can be useful to distinguish between two main types of PSBs: PSR dissolution imposed on an audience and audience-initiated termination of a relationship.

When Parasocial Friends Say Goodbye

The former category of PSBs encompasses a number of circumstances that can terminate a media user's PSR. First, the media content in which the beloved media figure appears can be discontinued such as when a person finishes reading the book featuring or the TV series starring goes off air or is canceled. Running out of new content featuring that media figure disrupts the PSR that the media user has cultivated for a prolonged period of time. Presumably, termination of television series is particularly consequential given the high levels of investment this media content often entails. In the days before binge-watching and time-shifting became the norm, viewers watched a single episode of a TV series at a time, at weekly intervals, season after season. In this way, viewers grew up with the characters and their PSRs evolved over the course of several years, sometimes a decade or even longer. Not surprisingly, then, when it is announced that a show is not going to be renewed for another season, its final episode can become a highly anticipated media event, drawing record viewership.

Famously, over 60% of American households, comprising over 100 million viewers, tuned in to watch the final episode of *M*A*S*H*. Aired in 1983, it continues to hold the record for the most watched series finale. The final episodes of *Cheers* (1993) and *Seinfeld* (1998) drew 80 million and 76 million viewers, respectively. Even in 2019, at a time when traditional television viewership has plummeted after decades of decline, the ratings of the final episodes of *The Big Bang Theory* (18 million) and *Game of Thrones* (19 million) rivaled those of the most popular shows from the 1990s and early 2000s, like *MacGyver* and *Sex and the City*. The interest surrounding shows' final episodes is also evident from Google search engine traffic, as searches for a specific series spike drastically around the time its last episode is aired (Lepori 2015, 35).

When a series is over, avid viewers become deeply distressed, as if they have lost a close friend. Their emotions range from sadness and anguish to emptiness and emotional numbness (Kottasz, Bennett, and Randell 2019). This emotional state, colloquially dubbed "post-finale depression" or "post-series depression," has even been linked to changes in investment patterns that have resulted in immediate diminished stock returns (Lepori 2015, 38–39).

A second way in which PSRs terminate involves the death (or departure by other means) of a character while the show continues. For instance, one's favorite reality show contestant can be eliminated and no longer make appearances on the program. At times, characters in a fictional series are written out, often as a result of failed negotiation for contract renewal for the following season or the actor's interest in pursuing other projects. For instance, T.R. Knight expressed his dissatisfaction with the screen time his character, Dr. George O'Malley, was receiving in the hospital drama *Grey's Anatomy*. This dispute led to his character's death in a car accident. Similarly, Dan Stevens's character, Matthew Crawley, was killed in a car accident in the third season finale of *Downton Abbey*, freeing the actor to focus on cinematic projects instead.

At times, exclusion of a character from the narrative is instigated by unforeseen events that require a rapid modification of the script resulting in unconvincing plot twists that lack proper closure. A recent example of such an unexpected turn of events was observed in the case of the 1980s–90s family sitcom *Roseanne*, which was revived in 2017. Just a few episodes after a very successful launch, Roseanne Barr, who played the titular character, posted an ostensibly racist tweet that resulted in the show's immediate cancellation. The sitcom was then promptly replaced by a spin-off series in which the rest of the fictional family continued the original show's narrative after Roseanne's character had supposedly died of an opioid overdose. Of course, in the context of celebrities (as opposed to fictional characters), PSBs can be caused by a real, not fictional, death. Some celebrity deaths are more foreseeable than others, affording fans an opportunity to come to terms with the possibility of an upcoming loss. For instance, extensive media reporting on Patrick Swayze's battle with cancer over the course of the last year of his life prepared media users for his death. However, more often than not, tragic, unexpected deaths put PSRs to an end abruptly, such as in the case of Robin Williams's suicide or Kobe Bryant's helicopter crash.

No matter the reason for the PSB—cancellation of a show or death of an artist—the strongest predictor of the intensity of PSB distress is the depth of the PSR prior to the breakup (e.g., Eyal and Cohen 2007; Cohen and Hoffner 2016). Bereaved audience members use various rituals and communicative strategies to process and cope with such a loss. They are guided by two main overarching goals that can be seen as somewhat conflicting: Seeking reconnection with the media figure and preservation of the relationship, and at the same time, coming to terms with the PSB and accepting the media figure's departure from their life.

Reconnecting with the Media Figure

The first objective of the mourning process is to reconnect with the media figure. Audience members relive their relationships through conservation of positive memories of the media figure and their PSR while editing out any negative aspects of the media figure's personality. To this end, fans can immerse themselves in media content featuring the media figure they are parting from. This includes both media coverage of the breakup itself (e.g., consuming news reporting on the celebrity's death and tributes to the deceased media figure) as well as consuming over again the original media content featuring that personality (e.g., listening to Michael Jackson's songs, rewatching Robin Williams's movies, etc.).

Fandom pilgrimage is another avenue for reconnecting with a PSR. Media audiences may travel to sites related to the media figure, such as filming locations, the site of the media figure's death, or stadiums and sports fields where the athlete used to compete. Fans can also attend memorial services or other fan gatherings that commemorate the celebrity, light candles, and bring flowers. There are countless examples of celebrity deaths that have left fans awash in collective grief—from scores of people, many of them female moviegoers, who attended Rudolph Valentino's funeral ("Public now barred at Valentino's bier" 1926, 1–5) to more than a million admirers of Princess Diana who gathered from around England and the world to accompany her on her last journey along the 3-mile funeral route (Brown, Basil, and Bocarnea 2003, 588).

At times, the media industry itself promotes events that facilitate such reconnection attempts (and that monetize grief and squeeze the last drop of revenue from loyal audiences, cynics would say). Often the finale of a popular television series is heavily promoted by broadcasters, creating a stream of media events building up to and following up on the airing of the last episode. For example, NBC accompanied the finale of the sitcom *Friends* with intensive promotional programming, including a two-hour retrospective and the appearance of the cast on the network's late-night talk show (Todd 2011, 6). In New Zealand, following the cancellation of the popular local show *Outrageous Fortune*, the largest museum in the nation opened a six-month-long exhibit devoted to the program, featuring the show's set, in-depth information about the characters, and videos about the show. The actors playing the main characters on the show attended the opening of the exhibition and interacted with fans (Russell and Schau 2013, 1045).

Furthermore, acquisition of memorabilia can be viewed as a way of symbolically holding on to a media celebrity (Russel and Schau 2013). Compulsive spending on show-related merchandise is directly associated with the intensity of media users' post-series depression (Kottasz et al. 2019). In such cases, desire to maintain the PSR through memorabilia is facilitated (or some may say, exploited) by commercial forces in the entertainment industry. An economic analysis of online auctions revealed that the soaring demand for celebrity memorabilia following a celebrity's death is typically met with a prompt supply response (Radford and Bolch 2013).

Another way individuals can cope with a PSB with a fictional character is to follow the actor who played that character to other media outlets. In so doing, media users are trying to sustain the relationships through other work of that media figure. Here again, the media industry facilitates this practice by producing "spin-off" series that develop secondary characters from beloved television shows into their own television programs. Others pay homage to characters that had a large following, in hopes of recruiting heartbroken fans to follow an actor to a new show. For example, Richard Dean Anderson was famous for playing the adventurous and creatively resourceful character MacGyver on the eponymous TV series. The character's name became synonymous with innovative ways of using tools and mundane objects to save the day (and the girl). Five years after the show ended with one of the most watched television series finales, Anderson played Lieutenant General George Hammond in the science fiction series *StarGate*. In the first episode of the new show, one of the characters addressed Anderson's character, saying, "it took us fifteen years and three supercomputers to MacGyver a system for the gate on Earth." This reference to Anderson's previous major role can be interpreted as a nod to audience members who followed the popular actor to his new show.

Finally, an important component of reconnecting with a media figure involves retelling stories about them. To this end, fans engage in various activities such as writing blogs, producing fan art (e.g., posting tribute videos of montages), and interacting with other fans on social media. Fan fiction plays an important role in this process as well, allowing fans to keep characters and their fictional universe alive long after a television series has ended. Fan-operated memorial pages are specifically created to commemorate media figures and offer space for communal grieving. Such online spaces provide mourners an audience with whom they can share these stories. For example, following the death of the legendary car racer Dale Earnhardt, fans connected online to recount their memories of attending his races (Radford and Bloch 2012). Congregating on social media memorial pages also involves maintaining the social image of the deceased media figure, thus contributing to construction of a narrative of their beloved personality as fans want to encapsulate it (Marwick and Ellison 2012, 393–4).

Finding Peace after a Media Figure's Death

In addition to trying to sustain a PSR, PSBs also involve coming to terms with the departure of the media figure. Mourning fans move toward acceptance of their beloved media figure's death and reconcile the identity conflicts it exposes. Here too, social media plays a particularly crucial role in the coping process by connecting mourners with same-minded individuals who offer emotional support and understanding that they often cannot find in their unmediated social environment. As one fan grieving the death of his beloved race driver, Dale Earnhardt, stated in his introductory post to the online community (Radford and Bloch 2012, 148):

> I just joined the list, in search of finding others who are as devastated as I am. Who understand this pain I am going through. Funny the first email I would get is about other people giving you funny looks, that is why I needed to find others who understand. [. . .] You can just tell [my colleagues at work] don't understand why I am so upset.

Online spaces, such as social media memorial pages are reserved for such expressions of grief and support. To enforce this norm, individuals engage in "grief police" practices, admonishing those who make comments that challenge the validity of fans' PSB experiences (Gach, Fiesler, and Brubaker 2017, 7).

Processing of a media figure's death is facilitated by the fan community. "Second screening" is a common practice in general, as individuals often use social media to communicate about what they are watching in real time. However, it is particularly crucial in the process of processing loss and dealing with a PSB. For example, live-tweeting spiked to particularly high levels immediately following the deaths of two of the most likable characters on the period drama series *Downton Abbey* (Schirra, Sun, and Bentley 2015, 243–4). This connectedness with others is critical as fans feel a deep need to share their experiences and emotions. One *Downton Abbey* fan recounted that she had known about the character's death ahead of other fans because she followed the show in the United Kingdom, where the finale had been aired before it was broadcast in the United States. The fan lamented that she had to cope with her grief alone, silently, unable to share her pain with other fans until the episode was aired in the United States (244).

Analyses of fans' online communication in response to the deaths of celebrities such as Dale Earnhardt (Radford and Bloch 2012) and Michael Jackson (Sanderson and Cheong 2010) demonstrate how these discussions allow individuals to slowly move from denial ("I refuse to believe that the King of Pop is gone," 334) to acceptance ("you are now in a better place where people can no longer hurt you," 333).

However, grieving over fictional characters can follow a slightly different trajectory. Elizabeth Cohen and Cynthia Hoffner (2016) comment on the unique challenges germane to the death of a celebrity versus a fictional character. The death of the celebrity is final and irrevocable. While it is still possible to find comfort in rewatching old content featuring the deceased celebrity, it is unfeasible to follow the actor in new media content playing new roles as in the case of a death of a fictional character. Nor is there a hope for the celebrity resurrecting as in the case of a fictional media character that can return to the screen in a reboot, flashback sequence, remake, or a plot twist revealing that the character actually was not dead all along. For example, according to the Eugene *Register-Guard* (1982, 1D) at the opening night of *The Wrath of Khan*, fans were reassured that although Spock had died in the movie, he would be resurrected. The producers followed through with their promise, bringing Spock back to life two years later in the sequel, *The Search for Spock*.

Hope for a fictional character's return was also evident from the trend of social media posts on Twitter following the death of Jon Snow's character on the hit television series *Game of Thrones*. Daniel and Westeman (2017) analyzed tweets posted over the course of two weeks following the unexpected killing of the very likable character Jon Snow. The researchers classified the posts according to the grief stages they expressed. To their surprise, the researchers found that rather than subsiding and giving way to acceptance of the character's death, fans' denial actually *increased* over time. In other words, viewers only grew more hopeful that the series's producers would bring the dead character back. Other research on television viewers' processing of season finales has similarly found that many viewers refuse to believe that a character (e.g., Sylar in *Heroes*) is truly dead and expect the deceased character (e.g., George from *Grey's Anatomy*) to somehow return to the show (Nabi and Clark 2008, 413).

Finally, the departure of a celebrity who constituted an important component in the identity and life of fans may require reorganization of one's identity. Fans often say that "part of themselves die" along with the celebrity (e.g., Courbet and Fourquet-Courbet 2014, 27). They can either reinforce this aspect of their identity ("I will forever love you") or switch interests, perhaps moving on to a different media figure who will help them redefine their identity.

In search for meaning in a celebrity's death, individuals may change their beliefs. For example, following the suicide of Robin Williams—an admired comedian who had struggled with depression—the actor's fans became more vocal advocates for policies supporting individuals with mental health issues (Cohen and Hoffner 2016). Others can find meaning in donating to social causes that the celebrity stood for during his or her life. For instance, following the death of the legendary basketball player Kobe Bryant in a helicopter crash in 2020, CNN invited viewers to "honor Kobe Bryant's legacy through the charities he supported" (Lee 2020). Indeed, an examination of trends in Google searches for two philanthropies that Kobe Bryant was associated with reveals a spike in searches immediately following Bryant's death even though the pattern of searches for each organization was very different during the rest of the year (Figure 10.1).

SAYING GOODBYE TO A PARASOCIAL FRIEND

In addition to PSBs caused by the departure of a media figure, PSBs can also be initiated by audience members themselves. Research on PSBs in young children has showed that PSRs last about two years until they are terminated by the viewer.

The most common reason for audience-initiated PSBs among children is outgrowing the relationship. Parents report that either their children begin to feel that their old media friend is too childish, or they get too tired of overexposure to their once favorite media figure. At times, children simply encounter a new media personality that captivates them, and their enthusiasm

Chapter 10

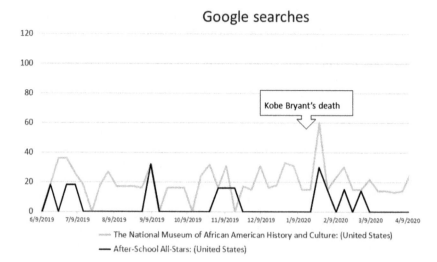

Figure 10.1   Google Search Trends for Two Charitable Organizations Supported by the Basketball Player Kobe Bryant, Who Was Killed in a Helicopter Crash on January 26, 2020. *Source:* Screenshot by author.

is redirected to the novel, exciting target (Bond and Calvert 2014). While this is likely to apply to adults as well, not all PSBs involve natural dissipation of a PSR. A more complex and potentially painful type of PSB occurs when a media figure disappoints their fan base.

Responding to a Media Figure's Transgression

Parasocial bonds are meaningful and therefore, as discussed earlier in the chapter, breakups come at great emotional and personal expense. From allegations of sexual assault against actors (e.g., Kevin Spacey) to doping accusations in sports (e.g., Lance Armstrong), to personal failures and dishonorable behaviors in one's private life (e.g., Tiger Woods's sexual addiction and marital infidelity), media figures' transgressions shatter their public image. For hard-core fans, the dissonance between the idealized image of the media figure and the media figure's misbehavior poses a threat to their self-identity and leaves a void in the space once filled by the parasocial bond. Thus, fan's response to a media figure's alleged misbehavior involves many moving parts (Finsterwalder, Yee and Tombs 2017). First, there are celebrity-related factors, such as whether the media figure denies allegations or takes responsibility, and how sincere their apology efforts appear. Second, there are media-user factors, especially the intensity of a media user's PSR with their chosen celebrity prior to the incident. The media user's value system and the nature of the transgression also play a role; some may deem illegal marijuana use a grave offense, whereas others do not find it problematic. Together, these various considerations contribute to audience members' meaning-making process, guiding their interpretation of the situation, such as making attributions about the media figure's responsibility. This process ultimately results in a media user forgiving their chosen media figure in order to preserve the PSR or leads to a breakup with the media figure when they have committed an unpardonable offense.

Two types of studies are used to empirically test this model's propositions, documenting the painful process that fans undergo when coping with a parasocial friend's transgression. In experiments, media users are asked to either (1) imagine a hypothetical situation or (2) read a mock news story. The imagined scenario or the fabricated news story involves their favorite media figure engaging in some sort of misbehavior. By carefully manipulating the different characteristics of these scenarios, such studies allow for pinpointing the considerations that media users factor into their judgments of their favored celebrity's transgression. However, these studies are divorced from the naturalistic context in which PSRs operate. One's response to hypotheticals or a single news story of questionable veracity might not be the same as one's reaction to a real-life scandal covered extensively by the media. Thus, in addition to experiments, surveys are also used to examine audiences' reactions to actual celebrity transgressions. Although it is harder for these studies to isolate specific causal factors that trigger different reactions, survey studies demonstrate how a celebrity's real past misbehavior relates to media users' subsequent feelings about that celebrity. Encouragingly, both surveys and experiments yield consistent results.

First, overall, media users do hold their parasocial friends to a high moral standard. In one study, Elizabeth Cohen (2010) asked college students what their response to a friend's or their favorite media figure's misbehavior would be. Students reported that misbehaviors would, indeed, significantly detract from their feeling of closeness with both a friend and a parasocial friend. Considering a variety of hypothetical scenarios, students indicated that they would be equally unforgiving of their favorite media personalities' and their friends' social misbehaviors (e.g., making inappropriate comments) and violation of trust (e.g., lying, breaking promises). However, moral transgressions, such as infidelity, driving while intoxicated, and physically assaulting others, would be even more detrimental to PSRs with a celebrity than to nonmediated friendships.

That being said, individuals do not take PSBs lightly and try to hold on to their PSRs. Although both major and minor moral missteps of a celebrity reduce PSR intensity, media users who have had a strong PSR bond with a media figure will try to rationalize that celebrity's misbehavior. Specifically, fans are more inclined to attribute misbehaviors to external causes, downplaying their favorite media figure's responsibility in a compromising situation (Hu et al. 2017; Osterman and Hecmanczuk 2020). They will also be more inclined to accept excuses made by the celebrity. For example, sports fans view drug violation as the gravest possible offense. However, they will be more forgiving of this misbehavior if an athlete's doping violation was motivated by preservation rather than acquisition motivations (i.e., preventing the injury from jeopardizing their career as opposed to trying to become the best in their field) (Lee et al. 2018). A strong prior PSR with a celebrity increases an individual's inclination to accept the celebrity's apology, deeming it sincerer, and believing that the celebrity is remorseful. In turn, acceptance of the celebrity's apology leads to preservation of the parasocial bond, and individuals report greater PSRs following the celebrity's show or remorse for their transgressions (Osterman and Hecmanczuk 2020).

In all, then, the outcomes of a celebrity's transgression depend on multiple considerations that media users weigh when trying to strike a balance between the motivation to preserve their relationship with the media figure and reflecting on the celebrity's damaged reputation. Consider, for instance, Michael Jackson, who during his life faced multiple allegations of child molestation, but nonetheless continued to enjoy his fan base's unwavering support. Jackson went to trial and was acquitted, yet allegations against him continued to resurface even after his death. When the controversy was brought up by media users on social media following Jackson's death in 2010, fans aggressively defended the star and silenced the provocateurs (Gach et al. 2017). In 2019, in the wake of the #MeToo campaign, the documentary *Leaving Neverland* was released. This film, which gave voice to Jackson's now adult accusers, shook some of the music artist's supporters, even within the industry. However, many of his fans remained tenacious and congregated on social media under hashtags such as #MJinnocent and #loveMJ. They used various strategies to cope with the threat posed by the movie and the surrounding public discourse. Now that the star is deceased and cannot defend himself, they reasoned, he should be allowed to rest in peace. Furthermore, fans called into question the credibility of the accusers. Some of them questioned the trustworthiness of the alleged victim and criticized his motivations. In sharp contrast, they described Michael Jackson's gentle and generous personality as evidence of the inconceivability of the accusations. Feeling as if they intimately knew Michael Jackson, even fans who had never met him in person felt certain that Jackson would never be capable of the crimes he was accused of.

Similarly, fans of the celebrated comedian Bill Cosby were shocked when sexual crime allegations against the star began to surface in the early 2000s. Their world was shaken again in 2018, following Cosby's conviction of three indecent assaults. Many of these fans grew up regularly watching Cosby play the role of a perfect father figure on the immensely popular, all-black television sitcom *The Cosby Show*. In his fictitious role as the patriarch of a middle-class black family, as well as his real-life persona—a successful black man in an almost exclusively White show-business industry—for many, Cosby was a source of inspiration and an empowering role model. Trying to reconcile this image with charges of rape and sexual assault, fans flooded Cosby's Facebook page, posting thousands of supportive comments under hashtags such as #FreeBillCosby.

FALLING OUT OF PARASOCIAL LOVE? HOW DO PSRRS END?

In surveys that I have conducted with Dr. Sam Dorros with adolescents and young adults reflecting on the PSRRs they developed while growing up, we saw that on average, teenagers' PSRRs lasted just over two years—which is strikingly similar to the typical duration of children's PSRs overall. In the national sample compiled for this book, PSRRs were on average a little shorter, just under two years. Participants in the survey were randomly divided into two groups: Half were asked to respond to questions about their most recent PSRR, and half were asked about their most meaningful relationship. Interestingly, the variability in the duration of PSRRs was tremendous, ranging from just a few weeks to decades-long relationships, but the average length of PSRRs was nearly identical for the most recent relationships (19.53 months, $SD = 45.85$) and the most meaningful ones (20.02 months, $SD = 34.06$). Importantly, however, in all of these surveys—whether involving college students, adolescents, or adults—PSRRs varied tremendously in length, lasting from just a couple of months to a decade or longer.

Why do romantic PSRs terminate? The research presented up to this point has examined the steps involved in and reasons for PSBs in general, rather than romantic breakups specifically. Up to this point, this chapter has reviewed research on PSRs overall rather than on romantic PSRs in particular. However, the same processes are likely, at least to some extent, to apply to all types of relationships with media figures. To shed some light on how PSBs work in romantic contexts, I have asked my interviewees about how and why their PSRRs came to an end. If their PSRRs were ongoing at the time of the study, I asked them what they anticipated could make them break up with their beloved media figure.

Outgrowing PSRRs

When presented with this question, some of those who were supposedly years past their PSRRs admitted that they had never actually stopped loving their chosen media figure. The "obsession" might have subsided, but it never entirely withered. These interviewees maintained that the media figure made up such a major component not just of their lives at the time of the crush but of who they are today that they would be forever intertwined.

Echoing findings from research on children, some individuals outgrow their PSRs, while others report that their PSRRs dissipate when a new object of fascination captures their attention. For example, Alex (interview #20) and Allegra (interview #24) had had many PSRRs. For Alex, the ones with television characters lasted longer—for several years at a time—because each show kept providing her with additional content to engage with, but the PSRRs with movie characters were relatively more short-lived because in the absence of new content, they dissipated within a few months, displaced by new parasocial romantic interests. Similarly, Allegra described her "obsessions" as several-month-long "binges" that brought a sense of "release" to the point that she "no longer fe[lt] this compulsion to find more stuff and watch them on YouTube, and watch their old interviews, and rewatch their movies repeatedly." Then, her PSRR would "kind of fade" and a new romantic parasocial target would grab her attention. She was rarely left "unattached" to a media personality.

In general, many interviewees attributed their PSBs to a substitution mechanism. PSRRs were terminated when they no longer fulfilled the compensatory purpose they had originally served. If a PSR has been used as a substitution for real social relationships, it loses its appeal when opportunities to form social relationships in one's close environment become viable again. For example, Alyssa (interview #10) said that her PSRR evolved when she was alone, "but when I'm in a relationship, I kind of have something," so she no longer needed a parasocial bond. Similarly, Flora (interview #8) recalled, "I started finding other guys attractive and, like, I was able to text like, other boys. I guess I was having more of like the real-life experience that I didn't feel like I just needed someone to fill up my time."

Forcing Oneself to Grow Up

For some, the shift from parasocial to seeking nonmediated romantic interests was not a smooth and natural transition but a conscious choice that followed from gaining a new perspective on one's own romantic PSR. This active decision to move on and graduate from a PSRR to embark on dating in the nonmediated world often came with three (related) realizations in what that has been described by Hunter (interview #15) as a "sobering up process."

First, it dawned on them that their PSRRs were futile. What had fueled their PSRRs all along was (a sometimes implicit) hope for a relationship with a media figure to transpire. But at some point the fans came to the realization that this hope was in some way delusional and unrealistic. Flora (interview #8) recounted how she went through this process together with her friends with whom she shared her romantic crush on the social media celebrity twins Grayson and Ethan Dolan:

> We had more of a reality that, like, we were probably never going to meet them. They were probably never going to fall in love with us. [Beforehand, we] really hoped it would happen.

With this realization came the motivation to shift toward nonmediated romance. Katherina (interview #9) came to terms with the idea that she had to move on when she recognized that her dream of a relationship with Justin Bieber would never materialize after Bieber got married "and that kind of made me realize like it's never going to happen, that I should snap out of it." Similarly, Alyssa (interview #10) admitted, "I kind of [. . .] had that realization after the movie—[. . .] I'm not talking to this guy. I need to talk to real guys that I can actually meet and whatnot."

Relatedly, after the realization that their PSRRs were not feasible, media users started questioning the adequacy of the PSRRs' places in their lives. Some interviewees came to the conclusion that that their PSRRs were overly obsessive, all-consuming, and interfering with their love life and other activities. Flora (interview #8) reflected on her infatuation and came to the conclusion that "it just felt unhealthy. I was like, why am I so obsessed with this person?" Mika (interview #11) also started to be more critical of the place and meaning that she gave the PSRR to occupy in her life: "I remember thinking at times I'm spending too much time doing [. . .] actually nothing—spending time doing actually nothing." Similarly, Hunter (interview #15) recounted:

> [I started] getting distance from that dream, finally starting to see that it was a dream, you know, and it's not real life and you can't just, I don't know, you can't just spend all this energy or headspace thinking that it actually exists between you and someone that doesn't even know of your life. They don't even know who you are, they don't even know that you're not a part of the universe.

Upon gaining this self-awareness of the unhealthy aspects of their PSRRs and how they were interfering with their social lives, these individuals made an active choice to put an end to their PSRRs. For example, Breanna (interview #7) explicitly sought to develop other aspects of herself apart from fandom and to cultivate romantic relationships in her immediate social environment:

> I was like, I should be going to the football games, like I should be going out and hanging out with friends more. I should be doing all that stuff, and then that's kind of when I started to realize, like, this is consuming me. I need to get ahold of myself and go experience the real world.

The Parasocial Lover's Betrayal

One reason for media-user-initiated PSBs discussed earlier is misconduct. As stated above, the stronger one's PSR is, the more likely one is to forgive their beloved media figure's misbehavior. The same applies to PSRRs. Cathy (interview #19), for example, told about her parasocial love interest, the lead of the band Iron Maiden, who left his wife for a young fan even after she supported him through cancer. Cathy admitted the unethicalness of his behavior: "Pretty crappy, right? Yeah, that's crappy. It's crappy that he left the wife that was there for him during such a tough time for him." However, when asked if she would have forgiven him, her answer was an enthusiastic "Yeah."

> I'd still take him. Oh, in a second. I'd [make him] leave that bimbo that's stolen [him] from his wife. [. . .] I would rescue him from her. [laughs].

As PSR research shows, media users often go to great lengths to defend their PSRs and avoid breaking up with a misbehaving media figure. The relevance of these elaborate justification processes in maintaining PSRRs became evident from my interviews with women who had romantic PSRs with Justin Bieber. My interviewees described him as a "pure, innocent boy" (Andi, interview #14) and a "perfect person" (Peggy, interview #13). I asked them how this perception squared with the very negative publicity that Justin Bieber had received over the years, including a DUI, assaulting a journalist, consuming illegal substances, and sexual promiscuity. The women I spoke to were poignantly aware of these transgressions, but rather than leading them to renounce their love for Bieber, the negative media coverage only made them hold on to their love interest even more. My interviewees resolved the dissonance by either dismissing the media reports as false rumors or finding excuses for his behavior. The attacks from the press and from individuals in their social circles made the fans feel that they were in a fight against the rest of the world, who misunderstood Bieber and by extension did not understand them.

For example, Peggy (interview #13) tried to maintain Bieber's image by discounting the allegations against him:

Whenever people would say like "oh, did you hear about this?" I would make excuses and say like, "oh, it's just the media, that didn't really happen". [. . .] Like he got a DUI and I was, like: "Oh the police are just like out to get him", like I doubt he was under the influence. Or: "It's just a media stunt," or something like that. [. . .] I saw him as such a perfect person, and I wanted other people to think like that too. And I didn't want people to badmouth him because it made me get like defensive and uncomfortable.

Brenna (interview #7) recounted her response to Bieber's scandals:

In 2013 he got caught up in a lot of scandals, and people from school would always say [. . .] how he was such a bad person and he was like not deserving of the things he has. Then I would just be so defensive, like, "No, he's such a good person." And I would try to dismiss the things he was doing as if it was okay, when [. . .] they really weren't okay. [. . .] They're really silly things. Like, he peed in a mop bucket and he was just like, really rude to his fans, and just the way he treated people was not okay. But for some reason, I tried to [. . .] justify it.

Her coping strategy entails what psychologists call "moral disengagement," wherein individuals do not apply their moral standards to their beloved celebrity. In an attempt to trivialize Bieber's misconduct, Brenna called his transgressions "really silly things" and used more sanitized language (being "really" rude) in reference to his alleged assault. These word choices consistently minimized the gravity of his behavior. When the allegations became more serious, she tried to find external attributions for his misconduct, suggesting that his behaviors were not a true reflection of his persona but a momentary response in an acute situation (e.g., stress). As such, they should be viewed as a temporary misstep rather than a flawed personality:

It was hard because [. . .] I knew that he was doing drugs and doing all these bad things that he shouldn't be doing, but [. . .] I couldn't—didn't want to let go of the perfect image I had of him. So I just like, defended him [. . .] everything he was doing [. . .]: "Oh he's just under stress, he has a lot of hate, it's fine." And it just wasn't okay but [. . .] [My friends and family] thought I was so crazy. They were like, this is not okay, like, he's doing really bad things. You shouldn't be supporting this. And I was like, "It's fine, like, he'll get over it. That doesn't make him a bad person, he's just making bad decisions and it's okay."

Similarly, Andi seemed to have found comfort in a documentary that enabled her to reframe Bieber's misconduct in a forgivable manner:

> He did a little documentary series on YouTube and he explained that entire process just how, like, being super famous, being super young, having access to so many things and like constantly having this amount of pressure on yourself and not being able to make mistakes, [. . .] he was just really going through it.

So what would it take for a celebrity to lead to a media-user-initiated romantic PSB? In my conversations with informants who were engaged in a PSRR at the time of the study, I asked them about a hypothetical scenario that would lead to a PSB. The responses varied, but there was an underlying theme of a break in trust and authenticity.

Both Damian (interview #17) and Ion (interview #2) struggled to come up with a scenario that would make them abandon their relationships. Damian described his PSRR interest as flawless for him. There was nothing she could do to change his way of thinking about her unless "everything she did was fake." Ion echoed this, saying that the only reason he could think of to break up with his PSRR target would be:

> Like if I found out that everything she [did], like all her songs weren't written by her, maybe? [. . .] Like if I found out that her whole persona was fake and there's [. . .] this other person or sort of team of people writing these songs and telling her what to do.

This actually did happen, eventually, to some of Justin Bieber's fans. As much as Andi (interview #14) and Peggy (interview #13) tried to defend his misbehavior and avoid a PSB, at some point the stretch was too much even for them. However, it was not the unethical behavior itself that was the relationship breaker for them. Rather, they describe the process of their disenchantment with Bieber as a break in his authenticity. In a move typical of romantic breakups in the real world, Peggy blamed the PSB on Bieber: "He kind of blew it up," she said, by breaking the image she had projected onto him. As Andi recounted, "I was like: wait excuse me, like who is this kid? [. . .] I just felt like I don't really know him anymore. [. . .] He's just not the guy I thought he was."

Finally, Gilli (interview #1) spoke about her expectations of reciprocity from celebrities. She expressed the belief that fans are the ones who support the celebrities and bring them to their standing, and thus they deserve celebrities' respect. Bringing up a K-pop group as an example, she described a hypothetical scenario that would make her break up with her crush:

If a group mistreats their fans, like sometimes they'll do a livestream, and think the camera is off so they start saying bad things about their fans. That would make me stop supporting them because they're putting up a front that isn't genuine, and not giving their fans the respect they deserve, because they are the ones who got them to where they are. Without their fans, they wouldn't be in the position that they are.

CONCLUDING THOUGHTS

Data from multiple surveys I have conducted consistently estimate the average duration of PSRRs at around two years. While there is tremendous variation around this figure, as some relationships lasting decades while others fade within a month, it is clear that individuals often experience PSBs. We also know that PSBs can be a painful process. However, little is known about the reasons leading up to PSRR dissolution or how individuals cope with PSBs. The processes of "sobering up" and "outgrowing the fantasy" that interviewees have described open the door to further new questions: What triggers this sudden shift from a latent hope in the possibility of the PSRR to a poignant realization that this hope is unrealistic and obsessive? How do individuals cope emotionally with this disenchantment? When a breakup can be anticipated, as in the case of post-series depression, how do fans prepare for it? And while there is much research on fans' grieving over a celebrity's death, it has yet to be discovered how these processes are similar or different from the experiences undergone by people who have had a PSRR with a deceased media figure.

Chapter 11

Concluding Remarks

Where Have We Been? Where Are We Going?

While the parasocial romantic relationships (PSRRs) as a subject of research has been overlooked for some time, it has been exciting to see it gaining traction as more studies examining PSRRs have been presented at conferences and appeared in scientific journals in recent years. My hope is that this book will contribute to these efforts by providing compelling evidence that PSRRs are an integral part of the social and cultural fabric and constitute an important aspect of many people's psychological experiences. It is argued here that PSRRs are deep, meaningful, and potentially highly consequential relationships that occur far more often and in more diverse populations than some have previously speculated.

However, beyond answering specific questions about the nature and consequences of PSRRs, this book is also intended as an opportunity to identify areas of research that have been understudied in the past and will benefit from further exploration. These research findings summarized in the book are used to outline the research agenda moving forward.

A RESEARCH AGENDA

Much of the PSRR research to date has examined demographic predictors of PSRRs and their consequences for relationship outcomes in nonmediated contexts. The review of the literature and additional research presented in this book offer several more promising directions for investigation: personality predictors of PSRRs, same-sex PSRRs, PSSRs across the life span, cross-cultural differences in PSRRs, and a macro-level look at PSRRs as a cultural and economic phenomenon.

Personality Predictors of PSRRs

Most past research has focused on demographic characteristics as predictors of engagement in PSRRs and PSRR intensity. However, this approach does not seem to have been very fruitful. Studies presented in chapter 3 consistently found that while PSRRs are relatively equally pervasive across various social groups, there is also a great diversity in the intensity of the PSRR experiences even among individuals who share demographic characteristics. This suggests that other individual differences, such as personality could serve as better predictors of PSRRs. Future studies could consider variables linked to social daydreaming and examine their applicability to fanciful romance as well. Such factors could include openness to new experiences and daydreaming styles. Just recently, Liebers and Straub (2020) took a first step in this direction, linking PSRRs with propensity for fantasy overall, and demonstrating the potential of this direction for further investigation.

Moreover, although media have not been around long enough to impact human brain evolution, it has been suggested that there may be biological heritable traits related to media processing that can also impact bonding with media figures (Stever 2020). The exploration of the biology of PSRRs and investigation of whether the propensity to engage in them has a genetic component is an exciting new frontier for PSRR research. Such biological and evolutionary mechanisms could potentially be used to explain sex differences in celebrity attachments in adolescence or changes in PSRRs across the lifespan.

Same-Sex PSRRs

Two populations in particular have been gravely understudied and need to be further examined in order to provide a more complete understanding of the PSRRs phenomenon—LGB and people aged 30 and above. Although the existing theorization of PSRR is not explicitly limited to heteronormative relationships, prior scholarship in this domain has not made special predictions concerning the roles of PSRRs in the lives of gays and lesbians. Nor has past research explored how heterosexual individuals may relate to same-sex media figures. Data gathered for this book suggests that same-sex PSRRs can be important component in sexual and romantic development of American adolescents.

It is not necessarily the case that same-sex PSRRs experiences are different from those of heterosexual parasocial romance—regardless of one's sexual orientation, PSRRs can serve as preparation or compensation for real-life relationships—but it is still worth investigating these experiences across the full gamut of types of relationships. In a broader sense, it is important to examine how PSRRs relate to "shiping"—a form of fan fiction in which media users imagine romantic (both same- and opposite-sex) relationships between characters that were not romantically involved in the original media text. Unlike imagines, a form of fan fiction that explicitly portrays the reader or the author as a character involved with the media personality (discussed in chapters 4 and 6), slash fan fiction depicts relationships between existing characters. However, it is conceivable that readers use slash to project themselves into the narrative and vicariously experience the PSRR with their loved character by psychologically merging with the fictional romantic partner in the narrative. Further research is needed to further examine how such indirect experiences, particularly through same-sex slash fiction, relate to PSRRs and the media users' sexual and gender identities.

PSSRs across the Life Span

Most of the theorization and research on PSRRs has focused on adolescents and young adults. Contrary to this stereotype, the survey data presented in chapter 3 clearly indicate that PSRRs can occur in all age groups, although the prevalence and intensity of PSRRs appear to diminish with age. There are several ways in which this finding can be interpreted.

1) *A cohort effect.* One explanation is that there may be a generational difference in how individuals relate to media figures. Millennials and Generation Y grew up in a media-saturated environment with fewer barriers to accessing media figures compared to Generation X and baby boomers. Of course, fandom was an important cultural force throughout the twentieth century—from the early days of cinema to Elvis Presley fans, Beatlemania, and Star Trek fandom communities. However, arguably, maintaining PSRs through fandom activities used to be much more laborious and required a greater investment of resources than it does today. Until the 1990s, fans had to acquire physical copies of video recordings of the media appearances and work of their favorite media figures. To connect with other fans and to obtain information about a media figure's private life, fans subscribed to print publications (from commercially produced magazines and newsletters to unofficial fanzines) and exchanged snail mail letters with other fan club members. Travel was necessary if individuals wanted to congregate with other fans and meet media figures in person.

Although fandom flourished and these fan activities were common, it is argued here that the Internet revolution substantially lowered the level of minimal investment required from fans. Information about media figures became readily available at little to no cost. If a fan in the 1980s had to spend hours (and many dollars) to obtain filmography books and then track down the video recordings of their beloved actor, a fan in the 2000s can gain access to all this information in a fraction of a second using a basic Internet search. Contacting a media figure used to be a complicated affair, starting with the sometimes nonstraightforward task of locating the celebrity's (or their agent's) physical mailing address. Today, many media personalities (including fictional ones) are easily accessible on social media platforms and invite fans to interact with them directly, thereby intensifying their fans' PSRs (Bond 2016a, 658).

To reiterate, fandom and PSRRs were pervasive and meaningful before the Internet era. However, the nature of PSRR experiences, on average, may have changed as a result of the dramatic drop in the minimum investment required to maintain these relationships. From a social exchange theory perspective, people's relationships with and commitment to media figures depend on their levels of investment in the relationship and the costs they endure to engage in it (Eyal and Dailey 2012, 771). Research examining both historic and current PSRR maintenance practices from a social exchange perspective—in terms of investment and costs—could reveal the impact that such investment shifts may have on generational differences in the parasocial romantic experience itself.

2) *An illusion of differences.* So far we have assumed that the negative correlation between age and PSRRs is a true reflection of age differences. Alternatively, it is possible that the negative correlation uncovered in the surveys is a social desirability artifact, wherein individuals misreport their experiences in an attempt to present themselves more favorably. According to this line of reasoning, PSRRs are equally prevalent and intense in all age groups. However, older individuals may feel less comfortable disclosing their feelings toward media figures because PSRRs are deemed less socially acceptable, and even stigmatized beyond adolescence.

I have noticed this firsthand in my efforts at recruiting informants through snowball sampling. Yong adults were eager to share with me their romantic parasocial experiences, whereas individuals in their thirties and beyond were more reluctant to do so. In several cases, young adult interviewees or other contacts referred me to middle-aged individuals whom they knew to engage in a PSRR. Yet, when invited to participate in the study, those middle-aged prospective participants either declined to be interviewed or ardently denied any romantic undertones to their fandom. It is therefore critical to destigmatize PSRRs by recognizing their prevalence and significance across the lifespan. Building on past PSR research, this book takes a first step in this direction. Chapter 8 offered a theorization of the evolving role of PSRRs at different points in people's lives, calling for additional research to validate some of these hypotheses and draw generalizations to larger populations.

A Cross-Cultural Look at PSRRs

Most research on PSRRs has been conducted in the United States (e.g., Tukachinsky and Dorros, 2018) and other so-called WEIRD cultures—Western, educated, industrialized, rich, and democratic—such as Germany (e.g., Liebers and Straub, 2020) and Israel (e.g., Karniol 1992). Anecdotal documentation of PSRRs in other cultures suggests that PSRRs are pervasive in East Asian cultures, such as the waifu and hasbado cultures in Japan and among followers of K-pop bands in Korea and neighboring countries. However, the exact prevalence of PSRRs in different cultures, their manifestation, the content of the social daydreaming involved in PSRRs, and the psychological consequences of PSRRs may be very different in these cultures.

Even within a given nation, there needs to be a more nuanced understanding of PSRRs in various subcultures. For instance, Asian American, Latinx, and black parents give their adolescent children very different lessons about dating and romance, socializing their children into different views of relationships (Stein et al. 2018, 612–3). Indeed, past research has shown that European-American and African American youth differ in the meaning and structure of their romantic beliefs (Weaver and Ganong 2004, 183–4) as well as their courtship norms, relational maintenance behaviors, and relational expectations (Braboy Jackson et al. 2011). It is reasonable to assume that these cultural variations will also manifest in differences in how individuals from different ethnic or racial backgrounds experience PSRRs. Although my surveys of US adolescents and adults discussed in chapter 3 did not reveal racial/ethnic differences in patterns of PSRRs, it is important to note that these data were not collected specifically with racial/ethnic comparison in mind. To explore ethnic and racial differences in a more direct manner, minority groups have to be oversampled. Additional questions specific to these groups' experiences can also be incorporated. For example, it would be important to understand how PSRRs intersect with group identity and cultural romantic and relational norms (e.g., PSRRs with characters of the same/other race or ethnicity). Much more research is acutely needed to better understand the role that culture plays in PSRRs.

Macro-Level Perspective on PSRRs

Finally, like past research on PSRRs, this book predominantly focuses on this phenomenon as a personal, psychological experience. However, as discussed in chapter 2, it is also important to consider PSRRs from the industry's point of view: How do celebrities respond to PSRRs? How does the media industry encourage, facilitate, and maintain them? In what ways do PSR benefit, harm, or transform the media industry? How do social changes inform these processes? How do economic and political forces shape the industry's practices pertaining to handling PSRRs? Such a macro-level approach would add another layer of understanding of the cultural significance of PSRRs and their social and historical contexts.

Appendix A

Survey Sample Description

The survey was conducted using a Qualtrics survey panel. The full sample included 566 respondents, of them 343 (60.6%) reported ever having a PSRR. Their age ranged from 18 to 90 years old, with a mean age 48.53 years old ($SD = 17.57$). The quota sample ensured diversity on key demographic characteristics. Table A1.1 presents the distributions for sex, race, educational attainment, and income.

Table A1.1   Description of Demographic Characteristics of General Population Survey Participants

		N	*Percent*
Sex			
	Male	258	45.6
	Female	302	53.4
	Other	2	0.4
	Missing	4	0.7
Race			
	African American/Black	67	11.8
	Asian or Asian American	66	11.7
	Native American	20	3.5
	Pacific Islander/Native Hawaiian	2	0.4
	White or Caucasian Non-Hispanic	327	57.8
	Hispanic/Latino	55	9.7
	Other	25	4.4
	Missing	4	0.7
Income			
	Valid Less than $10,000	42	7.4
	0 to under $20,000	44	7.8
	20 to under $30,000	52	9.2
	30 to under $40,000	45	8
	40 to under $50,000	38	6.7
	50 to under $75,000	125	22.1
	75 to under $100,000	76	13.4
	100 to under $150,000	83	14.7
	150 to under $200,000	32	5.7
	Over $200,000	26	4.6
	Missing	3	0.5
Education			
	Less than high school	12	2.1
	High school graduate	109	19.3
	Some college, no degree	127	22.4
	Two-year associate degree	63	11.1
	Four-year college	153	27
	Some postgraduate or professional schooling, no degree	19	3.4
	postgraduate degree	77	13.6
	Missing	6	1.1

Appendix B

PSRR Measure Used in the National Survey

BINARY MEASURE OF PARASOCIAL
ROMANTIC RELATIONSHIPS

Respondents were first asked to indicate whether they have ever had a parasocial romantic relationship (PSRR) using the following prompt:

> Some individuals have an experience of having a crush, falling in love or developing a romantic interest in a person they only know through the media. It can be a real person like a news anchor or celebrity or fictional character in a book, at TV show, a movie. Did you <u>ever</u> have such an experience?

- i. Never
- ii. Once
- iii. More than once

You have reported that you had a crush, fell in love or developed a romantic interest in a person they only know through the media. We will refer to this experience as a ROMANTIC INTEREST IN MEDIA FIGURES.

2. How old were you the <u>first time</u> you had a romantic interest in a media figure?
3. How old were you when you had the most <u>recent</u> experience of a romantic interest in a media figure?
4. How old were you when you had the most <u>meaningful/important</u> experience of a romantic interest in a media figure?

RANDOM ASSIGNMENT

Respondents who have indicated to ever have a PSRRs were then randomly assigned to one of the following sets of instructions:

1) Think of the romantic interest in a media figure that is most RECENT. Please answer the following questions with this experience in mind.
2) Think of the romantic interest in a media figure that is most MEANING-FUL AND IMPORTANT TO YOU. Please answer the following questions with this experience in mind.

Please answer the following questions with this experience in mind.

MEASURES OF GENERAL PSRR CHARACTERISTICS

5. The media personality's name: _____
6. Who was the media personality (if multiple apply, choose the one that best describes the role in which you were thinking about that media figure at the time).
   a. fictional character
   b. actor
   c. music artist
   d. athlete
   e. other media personality (e.g., news host, reality show contestant, youtube celebrity)
7. Tell us about the media you saw it in:
   a. Book _____
   b. TV show _____
   c. Movie _____
   d. Other _____
8. Sex of the media figure:
   a. Male
   b. Female
   c. Other (explain _____)
9. How old were you at the time you had this experience?
10. How long did it last for? _____ months ___ years
11. Take a moment to reflect on your experience. In a few sentences, please describe, why you were attracted to that media personality, what did it mean to you.

PSRR INTENSITY MEASURE

How did you feel towards the media figure? Please respond to the following questions based on how your felt at the time your interest in the media figure was the strongest. (Response options from "1" *Strongly Disagree* to "7" *Strongly Agree*):

   i. I was physically attracted to X
   ii. X fit my ideals of beauty/handsomeness
   iii. I imagined being with X sexually
   iv. I wished we could be involved in a sexual relationship
   v. My thoughts about X were romantic.
   vi. My thoughts about X were passionate.
   vii. I wanted X emotionally, physically and mentally
   viii. I wished X could know my thoughts, my fears and my hopes
   ix. I thought that X and I are just meant for each other.
   x. For me, X could be the perfect romantic partner.
   xi. X influenced my mood
   xii. I adored X
   xiii. I idealized X

RELATIONAL MAINTENANCE BEHAVIORS

12. Did you do any of the following (on a scale from "1" *Never* to "5" *Frequently*):
    a. Looked for X in the media (e.g., fan magazines, tabloids)
    b. Logging into X's website or following X's social media
    c. Imagined what it would be like to marry or be in a relationship with X
    d. Imagined X pick me out of a crowd and see me as special
    e. Thought about X in a sexual way
    f. Created art (videos, drawing, stories) about X
    g. Talk to a friend about your feelings towards X
    h. Talk to a romantic partner about your feelings towards X
13. Did you have a romantic partner during the time you had the romantic interest in a media figure?
    a. Yes, for all or most of that time
    b. Yes, for some of that time
    c. Not at all, or almost not at all
    d. Don't remember/not sure

Appendix C
Interview Sample

A snow-ball sample was recruited through word-of-mouth and through introductory communication courses at a medium-sized West Coast private university. Table A3.1 describes the participants' characteristics. All the informants' names have been replaced with pseudonyms to protect their confidentiality.

Table A3.1   Description of Demographic Characteristics of Interviewees

Interview No.	Pseudonym	Sex/ Gender	Age	Race	PSRR-Target Discussed in the Interview	Age at the Time of the PSRR
Interview #1	Gilli	F	19	Asian	Singer (NCTU, K-pop)	12
Interview #2	Ion	M	19	White	Singer (Alex Russo)	17
Interview #3	Cindy	F	19	Asian	Singer (Shawn Mendes)	18
Interview #4	Emily	F	19	White	Singer (Dong Srcheng, K-pop)	16
Interview #5	Nate	M	19	Asian	Character/actress (Princess Leia / Carrie Fisher in *Star Wars*)	Early childhood
Interview #6	Gina	F	30	White	Actor (Robert Downey)	20
Interview #7	Breanna	F	19	White	Singer (Justin Bieber)	9
Interview #8	Flora	F	19	White	Social media celebrity (Ethan Dolan)	12
Interview #9	Katherina	F	20	White	Singer (Justin Bieber)	13
Interview #10	Alyssa	F	20	White	Actor (Timothée Chalamet)	18
Interview #11	Mika	F	41	White	Characters (Edward from *Twilight*, character from *Queer as Folk*) and singer	31
Interview #12	Sierra	F	late 50s	White	Singer (Josh Groban)	40s
Interview #13	Peggy	F	20	White	Singer (Justin Bieber)	11
Interview #14	Andy	F	19	Asian	Singer (Justin Bieber)	12
Interview #15	Hunter	M	25	Asian	Character (Hermione from *Harry Potter* films)	13
Interview #16	Skylar	Trans-man	19	White	Character (Dean from *Supernatural*)	14
Interview #17	Damian	M	27	White	Actor (Anderson Cooper), singer (Sharon den Adel), anime character (Kikyou from *Inuyasha*)	13
Interview #18	Rochelle	F	73	White	Actor (Tom Selleck)	20s
Interview #19	Cathy	F	54	White	Singer (Bruce Dickinson)	15 and 51

Interview #20	Alex	F	19	Asian	Character (Magnus Bane from *Shadowhunters*), singer (Harry Styles), actor (Taron Egelton from *Kingsman*)	11 and 19
Interview #21	Adelyn	F	27	White	Tennis player, singer, actor	10–15
Interview #22	Mimi	F	21	Asian and White	Character (*Harry Potter* next generation), YouTuber (Connor Franta)	13–17, 20
Interview #23	Jessica	F	21	White	Characters (*Supernatural*, *Sherlock*), singer (One Direction)	12, 15
Interview #24	Allegra	F	43	White	Various actors	12, 15, 20s
Interview #25	Megan	F	24	White	Various fictional characters	
Interview #26	Ruth	F	38	White	Broadway actor (Allan Cumming)	36

Appendix D

Interview Prompts

The semi-structured interview was organized around the following questions, but each interview unfolded differently as additional deeper questions were used to probe the responses further.

- Have you ever been in love with, have romantic feelings towards, or had a crush on someone you knew from the media? It can be anyone like a celebrity, musician, actor, a fictional character in a book or a movie.
- Did it happen to you more than once? When was the first time? The most recent time? How long does it last for?

Tell me about the most recent experience. How did you meet (e.g., saw them in a movie/book)? Genre? How did you come across it?) (If a celebrity, what type of celebrity was it – athlete/musician/model/actor? How did you come across him or her?)

- Who was that media figure? How did you come across him or her at the first time?
- How did it happen that you realize you have a crush on them? For how long have you known that media person at that time?
  ◦ How did you realize this? How was it different from just fandom? How would you describe your feelings?
- Tell me about your life in general at that time. What was it like? Were you in a relationship?
- Did you ever feel jealous of the media figure's romantic partner (in real or fictional world)? Why?
  ◦ Did you have a crush on a media figure while engaged in a romantic relationship? Why do you think they can/cannot coexist?

- ○ Did your partner(s) know about your romantic interest in media figures? How did they respond? How would you feel if they had a similar crush on a media figure?
- What do you do? How do you experience the crush? How do you know you have a crush? What do you think? Feel? Do? Imagine?
  - ○ Did you do any art (creating videos, writing stories, paintings) related to the character? Tell me about it.
    - · What is it? What does it express? Why did you create it? How does creating it make you feel?
    - · What did you do with it once you create it? What did doing (and sharing) it made you feel?
    - · Did you share it with others? Why yes or why not? What feedback did you get from others and how did it make you feel?
    - · Can we have a copy of it for analysis? Will be allowed to display it?
- Did you talk to others about your crush? With whom yes or no? Why yes/no? What do they say? How does it make you feel?
- How does the crush impact your life? (good or bad things – brings you closer or more distant/conflict with others? Expands or reduces your activities? Makes you feel better/worse about yourself?)
- If you had a crush both on a celebrity and a fictional character – how are they different from one another in terms of your experiences?
  - ○ Is the character separate from the actor that plays them in a movie?
  - ○ How do you relate to the actor?
  - ○ How is it different from a crush on people in your actual environment? Did you have crushes on others in "real life"? How do they compare?
- What do you think makes you fall for a particular character/celebrity? What do you most like about him/her?
  - ○ Do the different characters share things in common?) Why do you think it happens when it happens? (Are you in a relationship? Going through things?)
- How did your experience with the media figure end? Why? When you have a media crush, what makes you get over it? How do you feel today about media figures you used to be in love with/have crush on?

Bibliography

Allen, Louisa, and Toni Ingram. 2015. "'Bieber Fever': Girls, Desire and the Negotiation of Girlhood Sexualities." In *Children, Sexuality and Sexualization*, edited by Jessica Ringrose and Emma Renold, 141–58. London: Palgrave Macmillan.

Alter, Cathy and Dave Singleton. 2016. *CRUSH: Writers Reflect on Love, Longing, and the Power of Their First Celebrity Crush.* New York: William Morrow.

Anderson, C. Alan, Jakob Camp, and Christopher M. Filley. 1998. "Erotomania After Aneurysmal Subarachnoid Hemorrhage: Case Report and Literature Review." *The Journal of Neuropsychiatry and Clinical Neurosciences* 10 (3): 330–7.

Andrews-Hanna, Jessica R. 2012. "The Brain's Default Network and Its Adaptive Role in Internal Mentation." *The Neuroscientist* 18 (3): 251–70.

Ann Landers. 1955. "Your Problems," *Chicago Sun-Times*, October 25. 36.

Aron, Arthur, Meg Paris, and Elaine N. Aron. 1995. "Falling in Love: Prospective Studies of Self-Concept Change." *Journal of Personality and Social Psychology* 69 (6): 1102.

Asendorpf, Jens B., Lars Penke, and Mitja D. Back. 2011. "From Dating to Mating and Relating: Predictors of Initial and Long-term Outcomes of Speed-Dating in a Community Sample." *European Journal of Personality* 25 (1): 16–30.

Ashe, Diane D., and Lynn E. McCutcheon. 2001. "Shyness, Loneliness, and Attitude Toward Celebrities." *Current Research in Social Psychology* 6 (9): 124–33.

Aubrey, Jennifer Stevens, Melissa Click, and Elizabeth Behm-Morawitz. 2018. "The Twilight of Youth: Understanding Feminism and Romance in Twilight Moms' Connection To The Young-Adult Vampire Series." *Psychology of Popular Media Culture* 7 (1): 61.

Bachen, Christine M., and Eva Illouz. 1996. "Imagining Romance: Young People's Cultural Models of Romance and Love." *Critical Studies in Media Communication* 13 (4): 279–308.

Bacon-Smith, Camille.1992. *Enterprising Women: Television Fandom and the Creation of Popular Myth.* Philadelphia: University of Pennsylvania Press.

Barbas, Samantha. 2016. *Movie Crazy: Stars, Fans, and the Cult of Celebrity.* Springer.

Barnes, Diana Lynn. 2014. "The Psychological Gestation of Motherhood." In *Women's Reproductive Mental Health Across the Lifespan,* edited by Diana Lynn Barnes, 75–90. Springer: Cham.

Bartsch, Anne, and Mary Beth Oliver. 2016. "Appreciation of Meaningful Entertainment Experiences and Eudaimonic Wellbeing." In *The Routledge Handbook of Media Use and Well-Being: International Perspectives on Theory and Research on Positive Media Effects,* edited by Leonard Reinecke and Mary Beth Oliver, 98–110. New York: Routledge.

Basson, Rosemary, and Willibrord Weijmar Schultz. 2007. "Sexual Sequelae of General Medical Disorders." *The Lancet* 369 (9559): 409–24.

Baxter, Leslie A., and Eric P. Simon. 1993. "Relationship Maintenance Strategies and Dialectical Contradictions in Personal Relationships." *Journal of Social and Personal Relationships* 10 (2): 225–42.

Bayle, Alfred. 2017. "Marriage to Anime 'waifu' Recognized by Japanese Company with Perk of Monthly Financial Support." *Lifestyle Inquirer.* November 23. Accessed September 21, 2020 from https://lifestyle.inquirer.net/279716/marriage-to-anime -waifu-recognized-by-japanese-company-offers-monthly-financial-support/

BBC 2019. "Why I 'Married' a Cartoon Character", August 16. Accessed October 22, 2020 from https://www.bbc.com/news/stories-49343280

Blake, Meredith. 2019. "How 'Game of Thrones' Wronged Its Female Characters in The Series Finale", *Los Angeles Times,* May 20. https://www.latimes.com/ entertainment/tv/la-et-st-how-the-game-of-thrones-series-finale-wronged-women -20190520-story.html

Blumer, Herbert. 1933. *Movies and Conduct"* New York: Macmillan & Company.

Bond, Bradley J. 2016a. "Following your "Friend": Social Media and the Strength of Adolescents' Parasocial Relationships With Media Personae." *Cyberpsychology, Behavior, and Social Networking* 19 (11): 656–60.

———— 2016b. "Media Use and Sexual Identity." In *The Routledge Handbook of Media Use and Well-being,* edited by Reinecke, Leonard, and Mary Beth Oliver, 422–33. New York: Routledge.

———— 2018. "Parasocial Relationships with Media Personae: Why They Matter and How They Differ Among Heterosexual, Lesbian, Gay, and Bisexual Adolescents." *Media Psychology* 21(3), 457v85.

———— 2020. "The Development and Influence of Parasocial Relationships With Television Characters: A Longitudinal Experimental Test of Prejudice Reduction Through Parasocial Contact." *Communication Research.* https://doi.org/10.1177 /0093650219900632

———— and Brandon Miller. 2017. "From Screen to Self: The Relationship Between Television Exposure and Self-Complexity Among Lesbian, Gay, and Bisexual Youth." *International Journal of Communication* 11: 94–112.

———— Brandon Miller, and Jennifer Stevens Aubrey. 2019. Sexual References and Consequences for Heterosexual, Lesbian, Gay, and Bisexual Characters on Television: A Comparison Content Analysis." *Mass Communication and Society* 22 (1): 72–95.

———— and Sandra L. Calvert. 2014. "Parasocial Breakup among Young Children in the United States." *Journal of Children and Media* 8 (4): 474–90.

Boon, Susan D., and Christine D. Lomore. 2001. "Admirer-celebrity relationships among young adults: Explaining perceptions of celebrity influence on identity." *Human Communication Research* 27 (3): 432–65.

Booth, Paul, ed. 2018. *A Companion to Media Fandom and Fan Studies*. John Wiley & Sons.

Braboy Jackson, Pamela, Sibyl Kleiner, Claudia Geist, and Kara Cebulko. 2011 "Conventions of Courtship: Gender and Race Differences in The Significance of Dating Rituals." *Journal of Family Issues* 32 (5): 629–52.

Brüne, Martin. 2003. "Erotomanic Stalking in Evolutionary Perspective." *Behavioral Sciences & the Law* 21 (1): 83–8.

Brunskill, David. 2017. "Learning from the Love Letters of Erotomania." *The Journal of Forensic Psychiatry & Psychology* 28 (5): 711–28.

Bryce, Mio, Christie Barber, James Kelly, Siris Kunwar, and Amy Plumb. 2010. "Manga and anime: Fluidity and hybridity in global imagery." *Electronic Journal of Contemporary Japanese Studies*. Accessed September 21, 2020 from https://www.japanesestudies.org.uk/articles/2010/Bryce.html

Busselle, Rick, and Helena Bilandzic. 2008. "Fictionality and Perceived Realism in Experiencing Stories: A Model of Narrative Comprehension and Engagement." *Communication Theory* 18 (2): 255–80.

Cantor, Joanne. 2013. "Why Horror Doesn't Die: The Enduring and Paradoxical Effects of Frightening Entertainment." In *Psychology of Entertainment*, edited by Bryant, Jennings, Vorderer and Peter, 333–346. New York: Routledge.

CeliaBowen (n.d.). *I Don't Care That He's a Fictional Character. I Still Want to Marry Him.* https://www.someecards.com/usercards/viewcard/MjAxMi02MGU zZGQzMDE3OTQ0NTc5/?tagSlug=movies

Chia, Stella C., and Yip Ling Poo. 2009. "Media, Celebrities, and Fans: An Examination of Adolescents' Media Usage and Involvement With Entertainment Celebrities." *Journalism & Mass Communication Quarterly* 86 (1): 23–44.

Cohen, Elizabeth L. 2010. "Expectancy Violations in Relationships with Friends and Media Figures." *Communication Research Reports* 27 (2): 97–111.

————, and Cynthia Hoffner. 2016. "Finding Meaning in a Celebrity's Death: The Relationship Between Parasocial Attachment, Grief, and Sharing Educational Health Information Related to Robin Williams on Social Network Sites." *Computers in Human Behavior* 65: 643–50.

Cohen, Jonathan. 1997." Parasocial Relations and Romantic Attraction: Gender and Dating Status Differences." *Journal of Broadcasting & Electronic Media* 41, (4): 516–29.

Collins, W. Andrew. 2003 "More than Myth: The Developmental Significance of Romantic Relationships During Adolescence." *Journal of Research on Adolescence* 13 (1): 1–24.

————, Deborah P. Welsh, and Wyndol Furman. "Adolescent Romantic Relationships." *Annual Review of Psychology* 60 (2009): 631–52.

Couch, Laurie L., and Allexa L. Koeninger. 2016. "Attraction: The Many Factors That Draw Us to Like, Lust, and Love." *Social Psychology: How Other People Influence Our Thoughts and Actions*, edited by Randal W. Summers, 299–314. Santa Barbara: Greenwood.

Courbet, Didier, and Marie-Pierre Fourquet-Courbet. 2014. "When a Celebrity Dies… Social Identity, Uses of Social Media, and the Mourning Process Among Fans: The Case of Michael Jackson." *Celebrity Studies* 5 (3): 275–90.

Crawford, Mary, and Danielle Popp. 2003. "Sexual Double Standards: A Review and Methodological Critique of Two Decades of Research." *Journal of Sex Research* 40 (1): 13–26.

Daily Telegraph. 2010. "South Korean Lee Jin-gyu 'Marries' Pillow Lover Fate Testarossa". May 16, 2010. https://www.dailytelegraph.com.au/lifestyle/south -korean-lee-jin-gyu-marries-pillow-lover-fate-testarossa/news-story/d9b3d474154 2b1df0c65c9ccc362e759?sv=9806c777fb8d9f923068b1655119b4ab

Daniel Jr, Emory S., and David K. Westerman. 2017."Valar Morghulis (All Parasocial Men Must Die): Having Nonfictional Responses to a Fictional Character." *Communication Research Reports* 34 (2): 143–52.

Davis, K. (n.d.) *Why MacGyver has Ruined Me for the Average American Male.* Retrieved September 6, 2020 from: http://www.postmodernvillage.com/eastwest/ issue16/16a-0004.html

Derrick, Jaye L., Shira Gabriel, and Kurt Hugenberg. 2009. "Social Surrogacy: How Favored Television Programs Provide the Experience of Belonging." *Journal of Experimental Social Psychology* 45 (2): 352–62.

———, Shira Gabriel, and Brooke Tippin. 2008. "Parasocial Relationships and Self-Discrepancies: Faux Relationships Have Benefits for Low Self-Esteem Individuals." *Personal Relationships* 15 (2): 261–80.

Dibble, Jayson L., and Sarah F. Rosaen. 2011"Parasocial Interaction as More Than Friendship: Evidence For Parasocial Interactions With Disliked Media Figures." *Journal of Media Psychology: Theories, Methods, and Applications*, 23 (3): 122–32.

Dietz, Park E., Daryl B. Matthews, Cindy Van Duyne, Daniel Allen Martell, Charles D. H., Parry, Tracy Stewart, Janet Warren, and J. Douglas Crowder. 1991. "Threatening and otherwise inappropriate letters to Hollywood celebrities." *Journal of Forensic Science* 36 (1): 185–209.

Dindia, Kathryn. 2003. "Definitions and Perspectives on Relational Maintenance Communication." in *Maintaining Relationships through Communication: Relational, Contextual, and Cultural Variations*, edited by Daniel J. Canary and Marianne Dainton, 1–28, Routledge: NY.

Dorsey-Elson, Laura K. 2014. "Twilight Moms" and the "Female Midlife Crisis." *The Twilight Saga: Exploring the Global Phenomenon*, edited by Claudia Bucciferro, 65–79, Scarecrow Press: Lanham, MD.

Driesmans, Karolien, Laura Vandenbosch, and Steven Eggermont. 2016. "True Love Lasts Forever: The Influence of a Popular Teenage Movie on Belgian Girls' Romantic Beliefs." *Journal of Children and Media* 10 (3): 304–20.

Drigotas, Stephen M. 2001. "The Michelangelo Phenomenon and Personal Well-Being." *Journal of Personality* 70 (1): 59–77.

———, Caryl E. Rusbult, Jennifer Wieselquist, and Sarah W. Whitton. 1999. "Close Partner as Sculptor of the Ideal Self: Behavioral Affirmation and the Michelangelo Phenomenon." *Journal of Personality and Social Psychology* 77 (2): 293.

Erickson, Sarah E., Sonya Dal Cin, and Hannah Byl. 2019. "An Experimental Examination of Binge Watching and Narrative Engagement." *Social Sciences* 8 (1): 19–28.

———, Kristen Harrison, and Sonya Dal Cin. 2018. "Toward a Multi-Dimensional Model of Adolescent Romantic Parasocial Attachment." *Communication Theory* 28 (3): 376–99.

Eugene Register-Guard. 1982. "Spock dies – but Wait! He'll be Back!", June 3, 1D. https://news.google.com/newspapers?id=kG8RAAAAIBAJ&sjid=W -IDAAAAIBAJ&pg=2635,627083

Eyal, Keren, and Jonathan Cohen. 2006. "When Good Friends Say Goodbye: A Parasocial Breakup Study." *Journal of Broadcasting & Electronic Media* 50 (3): 502–23.

——— and René M. Dailey. 2012. "Examining Relational Maintenancein Parasocial Relationships". *Mass Communication and Society*, 15 (5): 758–81.

Feeney, Judith, Patricia Noller, and Nigel Roberts. 2000.z"Attachment and Closer Relationships." In *Close Relationships: A Sourcebook,* edited by Clyde A. Hendrick and Susan S. Hendrick, 185–202. Thousand Oaks: Sage Publications.

Feingold, Alan. 1990. "Gender Differences in Effects of Physical Attractiveness on Romantic Attraction: A Comparison Across Five Research Paradigms." *Journal of Personality and Social Psychology* 59 (5): 981–93.

——— 1991. "Sex Differences in the Effects of Similarity and Physical Attractiveness On Opposite-Sex Attraction." *Basic and Applied Social Psychology* 12 (2): 357–67.

Finsterwalder, Jörg, Thomas Yee, and Alastair Tombs. 2017. "Would you for-give Kristen Stewart or Tiger Woods or maybe Lance Armstrong? Exploring Consumers' Forgiveness of Celebrities' Transgressions." *Journal of Marketing Management* 33 (13–14): 1204–29.

Fisher, Deborah A., Douglas L. Hill, Joel W. Grube, and Enid L. Gruber. 2007. "Gay, Lesbian, and Bisexual Content on Television: A Quantitative Analysis Across Two Seasons." *Journal of Homosexuality* 52 (no. 3–4): 167–88.

Floyd, Frank J., and Terry S. Stein. 2002. "Sexual Orientation Identity Formation Among Gay, Lesbian, and Bisexual Youths: Multiple Patterns of Milestone Experiences." *Journal of Research on Adolescence* 12 (2): 167–91.

Fortenberry, J. Dennis. 2013. "Puberty and Adolescent Sexuality." *Hormones and Behavior* 64 (2): 280–7.

Foster, Guy Mark. 2015. What to Do if Your Inner Tomboy is a Homo: Straight Women, Bisexuality, and Pleasure in M/M Gay Romance Fictions, *Journal of Bisexuality* 15 (4): 509–31.

Fouts, Gregory, and Rebecca Inch. "Homosexuality in TV Situation Comedies: Characters and Verbal Comments." *Journal of Homosexuality* 49 (1) (2005): 35–45.

Gach, Katie Z., Casey Fiesler, and Jed R. Brubaker. 2017. "Control Your Emotions, Potter: An Analysis of Grief Policing on Facebook in Response to Celebrity Death." *Proceedings of the ACM on Human-Computer Interaction* 1: 1–18.

Galloway, Lauren, Erika Engstrom, and Tara M. Emmers-Sommer. 2015. "Does Movie Viewing Cultivate Young People's Unrealistic Expectations About Love and Marriage?." *Marriage & Family Review* 51 (8): 687–712.

Gamson, Joshua. 2007. "The Assembly Line of Greatness: Celebrity in Twentieth-Century America." in *Stardom and Celebrity: A Reader*, edited by Su Holmes and Sean Redmond, 141–55. Thousand Oaks, California: Sage.

Garland, Malcolm, and Aidan McGennis. 1998. "Primary and Secondary Erotomania: Is the Distinction Worthwhile?" *Irish Journal of Psychological Medicine* 15 (1): 22–3.

Gerlach, Tanja M., and Selina K. Reinhard. 2018. "Personality and Romantic Attraction." In *Encyclopedia of Personality and Individual Differences,* edited by Virgil Zeigler-Hill and Todd Shackelford. Springer, Cham. https://doi.org/10.1007/978-3-319-28099-8_717-2

Giles, David C. 2002. "Parasocial Interaction: A Review of the Literature and a Model for Future Research." *Media Psychology* 4(3): 279–305.

———— 2010. "Parasocial Relationships." In *Characters in Fictional Worlds: Understanding Imaginary Beings in Literature, Film, and Other Media,* edited by Fotis Jannidis, Jens Eder and Ralf Schneider, 442–459. New York: De Gruyter.

———— and John Maltby. 2004. "The Role of Media Figures in Adolescent Development: Relations Between Autonomy, Attachment, and Interest in Celebrities." *Personality and Individual Differences* 36 (4): 813–22.

Glover, Jenna A., Renee V. Galliher, and Trenton G. Lamere. 2009. "Identity Development and Exploration Among Sexual Minority Adolescents: Examination of a Multidimensional Model." *Journal of Homosexuality,* 56 (1): 77–101.

Gomillion, Sarah C., and Traci A. Giuliano. 2011. "The Influence of Media Role Models on Gay, Lesbian, and Bisexual Identity." *Journal of Homosexuality,* 58 (3): 330–54.

Greene, Kathryn, Valerian J. Derlega, and Alicia Mathews. 2006. "Self-disclosure in Personal Relationships." *The Cambridge Handbook of Personal Relationships*, edited by Anita L. Vangelisti and, Daniel Perlman, 409–27, Cambridge University Press: Cambridge.

Greenwood, Dara N., and Christopher R. Long. 2011. "Attachment, Belongingness Needs, and Relationship Status Predict Imagined Intimacy With Media Figures." *Communication Research* 38 (2): 278–97.

Guo, Chiquan, and Chengyan Zeng. 2020. "Anime and Manga Fandom in the 21st Century: A Close-Up View." In *Handbook of Research on the Impact of Fandom in Society and Consumerism*, edited by Cheng Lu Wang, 480–96. IGI Global.

Hall, Jeffrey A. 2019. "How Many Hours Does it Take to Make a Friend?." *Journal of Social and Personal Relationships* 36 (4): 1278–96.

———— and Daniel Cochece Davis. 2017. "Proposing the Communicate Bond Belong Theory: Evolutionary Intersections With Episodic Interpersonal Communication." *Communication Theory* 27 (1): 21–47.

Halpern, Carolyn Tucker, Martha W. Waller, Aubrey Spriggs, and Denise Dion Hallfors. 2006 "Adolescent predictors of emerging adult sexual patterns." *Journal of Adolescent Health* 39 (6): 926e1.

Harrington, Lee C., and Denise D. Bielby. 2010. "A Life Course Perspective on Fandom." *International Journal of Cultural Studies* 13 (5): 429–50.

Hefner, Veronica, Rachel-Jean Firchau, Katie Norton, and Gabiella Shevel. 2017. "Happily Ever After? A Content Analysis of Romantic Ideals in Disney Princess Films." *Communication Studies* 68 (5): 511–32.

———, and Barbara J. Wilson. 2013. "From Love at First Sight to Soul Mate: The Influence of Romantic Ideals In Popular Films on Young People's Beliefs About Relationships." *Communication Monographs* 80 (2): 150–75.

Hendrick, Clyde Ed, and Susan S. Hendrick. 2000. *Close Relationships: A Sourcebook.* Thousand Oaks: Sage Publications.

Herdt, Gilbert H., and Andrew Boxer. 1996. *Children of Horizons: How Gay and Lesbian Teens Are Leading a New Way Out of the Closet.* Beacon Press. Ch 5, 173–203.

———, and Martha McClintock. 2000. "The Magical Age of 10." *Archives of Sexual Behavior* 29 (6): 587–606.

Herman, Edward, and Chomsky, Noam. 1988. *Manufacturing Consent: The Political Economy of the Mass Media.* Pantheon.

Honeycutt, James M., and James G. Cantrill. 2014. *Cognition, Communication, and Romantic Relationships.* New York: Routledge.

Horak, Laura. 2010. "Would You Like to Sin with Elinor Glyn? Film as a Vehicle of Sensual Education." *Camera Obscura: Feminism, Culture, and Media Studies* 25, no. 2 (74): 75–117.

Horton, Donald, and R. Richard Wohl. 1956. "Mass Communication and Para-Social Interaction: Observations on Intimacy at a Distance." *Psychiatry* 19 (3): 215–29.

Houran, James, Samir Navik, and Keeli Zerrusen. 2005. "Boundary Functioning in Celebrity Worshippers." *Personality and Individual Differences* 38 (1): 237–48.

Howat, Samantha (2020). *Gillian Anderson Made Me Gay: The Case of the X-Files Lesbians.* Thesis, Georgia State University. https://scholarworks.gsu.edu/sociology_theses/89

Igartua, Karine, Brett D. Thombs, Giovani Burgos, and Richard Montoro. 2009. "Concordance and Discrepancy in Sexual Identity, Attraction, and Behavior Among Adolescents." *Journal of Adolescent Health* 45 (6): 602–8.

Illouz, Eva. 1997. *Consuming the Romantic Utopia: Love and the Cultural Contradictions of Capitalism.* University of California Press.

Immordino-Yang, Mary Helen, Joanna A. Christodoulou, and Vanessa Singh. 2012. "Rest is Not Idleness: Implications of The Brain's Default Mode for Human Development and Education." *Perspectives on Psychological Science* 7 (4): 352–64.

Irving Shulman. 1967. *Valentino.* New York: Trident Press.

Jacobs, Arthur M., and Roel M. Willems. 2018. "The Fictive Brain: Neurocognitive Correlates of Engagement in Literature." *Review of General Psychology* 22, (2): 147–60.

Jenson, Joli. 1992. Fandom as Pathology: The Consequences of Characterization. In *The Adoring Audience: Fan Culture and Popular Media,* edited by Lisa A. Lewis, 9–0. London: Routledge.

Jenkins, Henry. 1992. *Textual Poachers: Television Fans and Participatory Culture.* New York: Routledge.

Johnson, Benjamin K., David R. Ewoldsen, and Michael D. Slater. 2015. "Self-control Depletion and Narrative: Testing a Prediction of the TEBOTS Model." *Media Psychology* 18 (2): 196–220.

Jozuka 2018 Accessed September 21, 2020 from https://www.cnn.com/2018/12/28/health/rise-of-digisexuals-intl/index.html

Juvenal 2018. *Juvenal and Persius* Edited and translated by Susanna Morton Braund. Harvard University Press.

Katayama Lisa. 2009. "Love in 2-D". *New York Times,* July 21, 2009. Accessed October 22, 2020. https://www.nytimes.com/2009/07/26/magazine/26FOB-2DLove-t.html

Karniol, Rachel. 2001. "Adolescent Females' Idolization of Male Media Stars as a Transition into Sexuality." *Sex Roles* 44 (1–2): 61–77.

Kawai, C., and Masahiro Sasaki. 2004. "Adjustment to Spousal Bereavement and Successful Aging: A 16-Year Longitudinal Study." *Shinrigaku Kenkyu: The Japanese Journal of Psychology* 75 (1): 49–58.

Kiser, Brett. 2013. *The Pin-Up Girls of World War II.* BearManor Media.

Kottasz, Rita, Roger Bennett, and Tom Randell. 2019. "Post-series Depression: Scale Development and Validation." *Arts and the Market,* 9 (2): 132–51.

Kretz, Valerie Ellen. 2019. "Television and Movie Viewing Predict Adults' Romantic Ideals and Relationship Satisfaction." *Communication Studies* 70 (2): 208–34.

Landers, Ann 1955. "Your Problems," *Chicago Sun-Times*, October 25, 36.

Larson, Reed W., Gerald L. Clore, and Gretchen A. Wood. 1999. "The Emotions of Romantic Relationships: Do They Wreak Havoc on Adolescents." In *The Development of Romantic Relationships in Adolescence*, edited by Wyndol Furman, Bradford Brown and Candice Feiring, 19–49. Cambridge: Cambridge University Press.

Lee, Lauren. 2020. "Honor Kobe Bryant's Legacy Through the Charities He Supported." *CNN.* February 21 https://www.cnn.com/2020/01/27/us/honoor-kobe-bryant-charity-iyw-trnd/index.html

Lee, Seung Hwan, Travis J. Simkins, Sean Luster, and Shahin Ahmed Chowdhury. 2018. "Forgiving Sports Celebrities with Ethical Transgressions: The Role of Parasocial Relationships, Ethical Intent and Regulatory Focus Mindset." *Journal of Global Sport Management* 3 (2): 124–45.

Leets, Laura, Gavin De Becker, and Howard Giles. 1995. "Fans: Exploring Expressed Motivations for Contacting Celebrities." *Journal of Language and Social Psychology* 14 (1–2): 102–23.

Lepori, Gabriele M. 2015. "Investor Mood and Demand for Stocks: Evidence from Popular TV Series Finales." *Journal of Economic Psychology* 48: 33–47.

Levinson, Daniel. J. 1986. "A Conception of Adult Development." *American Psychologist*, 41 (1): 3–13.

Levinson, Deborah S. 1997. "Young Widowhood: A life Change Journey." *Journal of Personal & Interpersonal Loss* 2 (3): 277–291.

Levy, Mark R. 1979. "Watching TV News as Para-Social Interaction." *Journal of Broadcasting & Electronic Media* 23 (1): 69–80.

Lilti, Antoinc. 2017. *The invention of Celebrity*. John Wiley & Sons.

Luo, Shanhong, and Guangjian Zhang. 2009. "What Leads to Romantic Attraction: Similarity, Reciprocity, Security, or Beauty? Evidence from a Speed-dating Study." *Journal of Personality* 77 (4): 933–64.

Marie Claire 2015. "The Ultimate Celeb Boyfriend Quiz" March 9, https://www.marieclaire.com/sex-love/quizzes/a4884/celeb-soulmate-quiz/

Malach Pines, A. 2001. "The Role of Gender and Culture in Romantic Attraction." *European Psychologist* 6 (2): 96–102. https://doi.org/10.1027//1016-9040.6.2.96

Malakh-Pines, Ayala. 2005. *Falling in Love: Why we Choose the Lovers We Choose*. Taylor & Francis.

Maltby, John, Liza Day, Lynn E. McCutcheon, James Houran, and Diane Ashe. 2006. "Extreme Celebrity Worship, Fantasy Proneness and Dissociation: Developing the Measurement and Understanding of Celebrity Worship Within a Clinical Personality Context." *Personality and Individual Differences* 40 (2): 273–83.

———, James Houran, Rense Lange, Diane Ashe, and Lynn E. McCutcheon. 2002. Thou Shalt Worship No Other Gods—Unless They Are Celebrities: The Relationship Between Celebrity Worship and Religious Orientation." *Personality and Individual Differences* 32 (7): 1157–72.

Mar, Raymond A., Malia F. Mason, and Aubrey Litvack. 2012. "How Daydreaming Relates to Life Satisfaction, Loneliness, And Social Support: The Importance of Gender and Daydream Content." *Consciousness and Cognition* 21 (1): 401–07.

Mares, Marie-Louise, and Gayathri Sivakumar. 2014. "Vámonos Means Go, But That's Made Up for The Show: Reality Confusions and Learning from Educational TV." *Developmental Psychology* 50 (11): 2498–511.

Martin, Karin A., and Emily Kazyak. 20090 "Hetero-romantic Love and Heterosexiness in Children's G-rated Films." *Gender & Society* 23 (3): 315–36.

Marwick, Alice, and Nicole B. Ellison. 2012. "There isn't Wifi in Heaven! Negotiating Visibility on Facebook Memorial Pages." *Journal of Broadcasting & Electronic Media* 56, (3): 378–400.

Marwit, Samuel J., and Dennis Klass. 1995. "Grief and the Role of the Inner Representation of the Deceased." *Omega-Journal of Death and Dying* 30, (4): 283–98.

Mayer, Jacob Peter. 1946. *Sociology of Film: Studies and Documents*. Faber.

———. 1948. *British Cinemas and Their Audiences*. Ayer Publishing.

McCutcheon, Lynn E., Rense Lange, and James Houran. 2002. "Conceptualization and Measurement of Celebrity Worship." *British Journal of Psychology* 93 (1): 67–87.

McDayter, Ghislaine. 2009. *Byromania and the Birth of Celebrity Culture*. Suny Press.

McMillan, Rebecca, Scott Barry Kaufman, and Jerome L. Singer. 2013 "Ode to Positive Constructive Daydreaming." *Frontiers in Psychology* 4: 626.

Meloy, J. R. (1998). *The Psychology of Stalking: Clinical and Forensic Perspectives.* San Diego: Academic Press.

Merolla, Andy J. 2010. "Relational Maintenance During Military Deployment: Perspectives of Wives of Deployed US Soldiers." *Journal of Applied Communication Research* 38 (1): 4–26.

Moser, Charles, and Peggy J. Kleinplatz. 2006. "DSM-IV-TR and the Paraphilias: an Argument for Removal." *Journal of Psychology & Human Sexuality* 17 (3/4): 91–109.

Mullen, Paul E., and Michele Pathé. 1994. "The Pathological Extensions of Love." *British Journal of Psychiatry* 165 (5): 614–63.

Mulligan, K. (2018). "Media Ownership Concentration and Minority Representation in Prime Time Entertainment Television." In *The Hollywood Connection: The Influence of Fictional Media and Celebrity Politics on American Public Opinion*, edited by Timothy G. Hill, and Heather E. Yates, 17–34. New York: Lanham Maryland Lexington Books.

Nabi, Robin L., and Shannon Clark. 2008. "Exploring the Limits of Social Cognitive Theory: Why Negatively Reinforced Behaviors on TV May Be Modeled Anyway." *Journal of Communication* 58 (3): 407–27.

NBC Nightly News. 2016. "Simone Biles Takes Nightly News Inside Her Home." April 9, Video, 00:00:32. https://www.nbcnews.com/nightly-news/video/u-s-olym-pic-gymnast-simone-biles-takes-nightly-news-inside-her-home-740915267766

Nussbaum, Felicity. 2010. *Rival Queens: Actresses, Performance, and the Eighteenth-Century British Theater.* Philadelphia: University of Pennsylvania Press.

Nisbet, Erik C., and Teresa A. Myers. 2012. "Cultivating Tolerance of Hmosexuals." In *Living With Television Now: Advances in Cultivation Theory & Research*, edited by Morgan, Michael, James Shanahan, and Nancy Signorielli, 61–80. New York: Peter Lang.

Norris (n.d.). *Who Was the Lonesome Gal with the Mask?* https://www.rusc.com/old -time-radio/articles/Who-was-the-lonesome-gal-with-the-mask-.aspx?id=595

Öhman, Arne, and Joaquim J. Soares. 1993. "On the Automatic Nature of Phobic Fear: Conditioned Electrodermal Responses to Masked Fear-Relevant Stimuli." *Journal of Abnormal Psychology* 102 (1): 121–32.

Olderbak, Sally G., Frederic Malter, Pedro Sofio Abril Wolf, Daniel N. Jones, and Aurelio José Figueredo. 2017. "Predicting Romantic Interest at Zero Acquaintance: Evidence of Sex Differences in Trait Perception but Not in Predictors of Interest." *European Journal of Personality* 31 (1): 42–62.

Ortiz, Michelle, and Jake Harwood. 2007. "A Social Cognitive Theory Approach to the Effects of Mediated Intergroup Contact on Intergroup Attitudes." *Journal of Broadcasting & Electronic Media* 51 (4): 615–31.

Osterman, Lindsey L., and Theresa A. Hecmanczuk. 2020. "Parasocial Forgiveness: The Roles of Parasocial Closeness and Offense Perceptions." *Journal of Social and Personal Relationships* 37 (3): 800–20.

Patterson, Genell E., David B. Ward, and Tiffany B. Brown. 2003. "Relationship Scripts: How Young Women Develop and Maintain Same-Sex Romantic Relationships." *Journal of GLBT Family Studies* 9 (2): 179–201.

Perun, Maria B., 2013. "Maternal Identity of Women in the Postpartum Period." *The Journal of Education, Culture, and Society* 4 (1): 95–105.

Pines, Ayala M. 1998. "A prospective Study of Personality and Gender Differences in Romantic Attraction." *Personality and Individual Differences* 25 (1): 147–57.

Poerio, Giulia Lara, and Jonathan Smallwood. 2016. "Daydreaming to Navigate the Social World: What We Know, What We Don'' Know, and Why it Matters." *Social and Personality Psychology Compass* 10 (11): 605–18.

———, Peter Totterdell, Lisa-Marie Emerson, and Eleanor Miles. 2016. "Social Daydreaming and Adjustment: An Experience-Sampling Study of Socio-Emotional Adaptation During a Life Transition." *Frontiers in Psychology* 7(13): 1664–78.

"Public Now Barred at Valentino's Bier." 1926. *New York Times,* August 26. 1, 5

Puente, Maria (2015). "John Lennon's Ex-wife, Cynthia Lennon, Dies." *USA Today,* April 1, https://www.usatoday.com/story/life/music/2015/04/01/john-lennons-ex-wife-cynthia-lennon-dies/70770278/

Radford, Scott K., and Peter H. Bloch. 2012. "Grief, Commiseration, and Consumption Following the Death of a Celebrity." *Journal of Consumer Culture,* 12(2): 137–55.

Radway, Janice A. 2009. *Reading the Romance: Women, patriarchy, and Popular Literature.* University of North Carolina Press.

Raley, Amber B., and Jennifer L. Lucas. 2006. "Stereotype or Success? Prime-time Television's Portrayals of Gay Male, Lesbian, And Bisexual Characters." *Journal of Homosexuality* 51 (2): 19–38.

Reeves, Byron and Clifford Naas. 1996. *The Media Equation.* Cambridge Press.

Reeves, Robert A., Gary A. Baker, and Chris S. Truluck. 2012. "Celebrity Worship, Materialism, Compulsive Buying, and The Empty Self." *Psychology & Marketing* 29 (9): 674–79.

Regan, Pamela C., Lauren Levin, Susan Sprecher, F. Scott Christopher, and Rodney Gate. 2000. "Partner Preferences: What Characteristics do Men and Women Desire in Their Short-Term Sexual and Long-Term Romantic Partners?." *Journal of Psychology & Human Sexuality* 12 (3): 1–21.

Rosaen, Sarah F., and Jayson L. Dibble. 2016. "Clarifying the Role of Attachment and Social Compensation on Parasocial Relationships with Television Characters." *Communication Studies* 67 (2): 147–162.

Rosario, Margaret, Eric W. Schrimshaw, and Joyce Hunter. 2008. "Predicting Different Patterns of Sexual Identity Development Over Time Among Lesbian, Gay, and Bisexual Youths: A Cluster Analytic Approach." *American Journal of Community Psychology* 42 (3–4): 266–82.

Rubin, Alan M., Elizabeth M. Perse, and Robert A. Powell. 1985. "Loneliness, Parasocial Interaction, and Local Television News Viewing." *Human Communication Research* 12 (2): 155–80.

Russell, Cristel Antonia, and Hope Jensen Schau. 2014. "When Narrative Brands End: The Impact of Narrative Closure and Consumption Sociality on Loss Accommodation." *Journal of Consumer Research* 40 (6): 1039–62.

Russo, Julie Levin. 2013. "Queer Female Fandom Online." in *The Routledge Companion to Media & Gender* edited by Cynthia Carter, 450–61. New York: Routledge.

Sae, Kitamura. "The Role of Women in the Canonisation of Shakespeare: From Elizabethan Theatre to the Shakespeare Jubilee." PhD diss., King's College London, 2013.

Salmon, Catherine, and Don Symons.2001. "Slash Fiction and Human Mating Psychology." *Journal of Sex Research* 41 (1): 94–100.

Sanderson, Jimmy, and Pauline Hope Cheong. 2010. "Tweeting Prayers and Communicating Grief over Michael Jackson Online." *Bulletin of Science, Technology & Society* 30 (5): 328–40.

Saunders, Rhonda, and Sean L. Wainwright. 2008. "Prosecuting Celebrity Stalkers." *Stalking, Threatening, and Attacking Public Figures: A Psychological and Behavioral Analysis,* 407 ch 2. Oxford University Press.

Savin-Williams, Ritch C., and Kenneth M. Cohen. 2015. "Developmental Trajectories and Milestones of Lesbian, Gay, And Bisexual Young People." *International Review of Psychiatry* 27 (5): 357–66.

Schirra, Steven, Huan Sun, and Frank Bentley. 2014. "Together Alone: Motivations for Live-Tweeting a Television Series." *Proceedings of The Sigchi Conference On Human Factors in Computing Systems*: 2441–2450, Association for Computing Machinery: NYs. https://dl.acm.org/doi/proceedings/10.1145/2556288

Schneider, Danielle S., Paul A. Sledge, Stephen R. Shuchter, and Sidney Zisook. 1996. "Dating and Remarriage Over the First Two Years of Widowhood." *Annals of Clinical Psychiatry* 8 (2): 51–57.

Schneiderman, Inna, Orna Zagoory-Sharon, James F. Leckman, and Ruth Feldman. 2012. "Oxytocin During the Initial Stages of Romantic Attachment: Relations to Couples' Interactive Reciprocity." *Psychoneuroendocrinology* 37 (8): 1277–85.

Scott, John T., ed. 2006. *Jean-Jacques Rousseau: Politics, Art, and Autobiography*. Taylor & Francis.

Scott, Suzanne. 2015. "The Moral Economy of Crowdfunding and the Transformative Capacity of Fan-ancing." *New Media & Society* 17 (2): 167–182.

Sigman, Stuart J. 1991. "Handling the Discontinuous Aspects of Continuous Social Relationships: Toward Research on The Persistence of Social Forms." *Communication Theory* 1 (2): 106–27.

Slater, Michael D., Benjamin K. Johnson, Jonathan Cohen, Maria Leonora G. Comello, and David R. Ewoldsen. 2014. "Temporarily Expanding the Boundaries of the self: Motivations for Entering the story World and Implications for Narrative Effects." *Journal of Communication* 64 (3): 439–55.

Smith, Emma. 1919. "Fandom, Women and the Shakespearean Theater." YouTube video, from *Creating a Climate of Change* series at the Said Business School, University of Oxford February 22, 2019. Posted Saïd Business School, University of Oxford, May 14, 2019, YouTube video, 01:06:04, https://www.youtube.com/watch?v=tbvEXRBGYcE

Stein, Gabriela L., Stephanie I. Coard, Lisa Kiang, Ruth K. Smith, and Yesenia C. Mejia. 2018. "The Intersection of Racial–Ethnic Socialization and Adolescence: A Closer Examination at Stage-Salient Issues." *Journal of Research on Adolescence* 28 (3): 609–21.

Stafford, Laura. 2003. "Maintaining Romantic Relationships: Summary and Analysis of One Research Program." in *Maintaining Relationships Through Communication: Relational, Contextual, and Cultural Variations*, edited by Daniel J. Canary and Marianne Dainton, 51–77. New York: Routledge.

Stern, Daniel. 1995. *The Motherhood Constellation: A Unified View of Parent–Infant Psychotherapy*. New York: Basic Books.

———— and Bruschweiler-Stern, Nadia. 1998. *The Birth of a Mother: How The Motherhood Experience Changes You Forever*. New York: Basic Books.

Stever, Gayle S. 2009. "Parasocial and Social Interaction with Celebrities: Classification of Media Fans." *Journal of Media Psychology* 14 (3): 1–39.

———— 2011. "Fan Behavior and Lifespan Development Theory: Explaining Para-Social and Social Attachment to Celebrities." *Journal of Adult Development* 18 (1): 1–7.

———— 2017. "Evolutionary Theory and Reactions to Mass Media: Understanding Parasocial Attachment." *Psychology of Popular Media Culture* 6(2): 95–102.

———— 2018. *The Psychology of Celebrity*. New York: Routledge.

———— 2020. "Evolutionary Psychology and Mass Media". In *The Sage Handbook of Evolutionary Psychology: Applications of Evolutionary Psychology,* edited by Todd K. Shackelford, 398–416. New York: Sage.

Tal-Or, Nurit, and Yael Papirman. 2007. "The Fundamental Attribution Error in Attributing Fictional Figures' Characteristics to The Actors." *Media Psychology* 9 (2): 331–45.

Tsao, Jinshi. 1996. "Compensatory Media Use: An Exploration of two Paradigms." *Communication Studies* 47 (1–2): 89–109.

TrueCloud9999 2010. "Marriage Between a Korean Otaku and a Pillowcase (Dakimakura) of an Anime Character" May 5, 2010, YouTube video, 5:00, https://www.youtube.com/watch?v=dUIOgd2JQJc

Tuite, Clara. 2015. *Lord Byron and scandalous Celebrity*. Cambridge University Press.

Tukachinsky, Riva. 2010. "Para-Romantic Love and Para-Friendships: Development and Assessment of a Multiple-Parasocial Relationships Scale." *American Journal of Media Psychology* 3 (1/2): 73–94.

———— 2020. "Playing a Bad Character but Endorsing a Good Cause: Actor-Character Fundamental Attribution Error and Persuasion." *Communication Reports 33* (1): 1–13.

———— and Sybilla M. Dorros. 2017. *Adolescent Parasocial Romantic Relationships and Initial Sexual Development, Fantasies, and Dating Experiences*. Paper presented at the International Communication Association Annual Convention, San Diego, CA.

———— and Sybilla M. Dorros. 2018. "Parasocial Romantic Relationships, Romantic Beliefs, And Relationship Outcomes in USA Adolescents: Rehearsing Love or Setting Oneself Up to Fail?." *Journal of Children and Media* 12 (3): 329–45.

————, Holke Inaba, Kristina Kraus, Dominique Stewart, and Michelle Williams. 2019. "Sex, likes and Instagram: Celebrity Self-presentation on Instagram Images." In *How Celebrity Lives Affect Our Own: Understanding the Impact on*

Americans' Public and Private Lives, edited by Carol Madere, 165–79. Rowman & Littlefield.

———— and Gayle Stever. 2019. Theorizing Development of Parasocial Engagement." *Communication Theory* 29 (3): 297–318.

————, Walter, N., and Saucier, C. (2020). Antecedents and Effects of Parasocial Relationships: A Meta-Analysis. *Journal of Communication* 70 (60). https://doi .org/10.1093/joc/jqaa034

Tuominen, Jarno, Tuula Stenberg, Antti Revonsuo, and Katja Valli. 2019. "Social Contents in Dreams: An Empirical Test of the Social Simulation Theory." *Consciousness and Cognition* 69: 133–45.

Tuval-Mashiach, Rivka, Sophie Walsh, Shirley Harel, and Shmuel Shulman. 2008. "Romantic Fantasies, Cross-Gender Friendships, and Romantic Experiences in Adolescence." *Journal of Adolescent Research* 23 (4): 471–87.

Vermorel, Fred. 2011. *Starlust: The Secret Fantasies of Fans*. Faber & Faber.

Vice (2018). "The Story Behind That Guy Who Married an Anime Hologram in Japan" *Vice,* November 14. https://www.vice.com/en_us/article/nepbgx/the-story -behind-that-guy-who-married-an-anime-hologram-in-japan

Ward, L. Monique, Kyla M. Day, and Marina Epstein. 2006. "Uncommonly Good: Exploring How Mass Media May Be a Positive Influence on Young Women's Sexual Health and Development." *New Directions for Child and Adolescent Development*, 112: 57–70.

Weaver, Shannon E., and Lawrence H. Ganong. "The Factor Structure of the Romantic Beliefs Scale for African Americans and European Americans." *Journal of Social and Personal Relationships 21* (2): 171–85.

Weinstein, Deena. 1999. "Art Versus Commerce: Deconstructing A (Useful) Romantic Illusion." In *Stars Don't Stand Still in The Sky: Music and Myth,* edited by Karen Kelly and Evelyn McDonnell, 56–69. New York: New York University Press.

Whitten, Sarah. 2019. 'Game of Thrones' Faffe: Coffee Cup Left in Final Cut of Episode 4." *CNN,* May 7 2019 https://www.cnbc.com/2019/05/06/game-of-thrones -gaffe-starbucks-cup-left-in-final-cut-of-episode-4.html

Yahoo Answers (n.d.). "I Have a Crush On Holden Caulfield from Catcher in The Rye...?" https://answers.yahoo.com/question/index?qid=20170419001654A APwEWz

Yule, Morag A., Lori A. Brotto, and Boris B. Gorzalka. 2017. "Sexual Fantasy and Masturbation Among Asexual Individuals: An In-Depth Exploration." *Archives of Sexual Behavior* 46 (1): 311–328.

Index

Page references for figures are italicized

About the Author

Rebecca (Riva) Tukachinsky Forster (PhD) is an associate professor in the School of Communication at Chapman University. Her research program examines psychological involvement with media, particularly how individuals relate to and are ultimately impacted by celebrities and fictional characters. Her work on parasocial relationships has been published in the *Journal of Communication, Communication Theory, Mass Communication and Society, Annals of Communication*, and *Journal of Children and Media.*

Milton Keynes UK
Ingram Content Group UK Ltd.
UKHW021324170823
427036UK00023B/718